Sea of Ghosts

Winterhold

Windhelm

Blacklight

Gnisis

Riften

edge of the world

Bruma

Vvardenfell

Dagon Fel

Firewatch

Redmountain

Ald'ruhn

Balmora

Sadrith Mora

Seyda Neen

Vivec

Necrom

Cheydinhal

Morrowind

Imperial City

Mournhold

Narsis

Tear

Niben bay

Bravil

Stormhold

Thorn

rverhold

rcrest

Rimmen

Black Marsh

sweyr

Helstrom

orinthe

Gideon

Larawiin

Tenmar forest

rval

Topal bay

Archon

Senchal

Soulrest

Blackrose

Lilmoth

The Padomaic Ocean

The Elder Scrolls®

THE OFFICIAL COOKBOOK

The Elder Scrolls®

THE OFFICIAL COOKBOOK

Recipes from Skyrim®, Morrowind, and across Tamriel

By Chelsea Monroe-Cassel

Titan BOOKS

London

An Insight Editions Book

CONTENTS

DEAD MAN'S DRINK

INTRODUCTION

I used to be an adventurer . . .

Oh, you've heard that story already?

It's remarkable how familiar tales can become something fresh with just a little tweaking. Recipes are much the same. They can be gathered as one travels then adapted to suit the season, location, or what's available in your home larder.

When it comes to selecting your ingredients, it's important to be a little flexible. These recipes are reflective of the basic recipes found across Skyrim, Morrowind, and the whole of Tamriel, but should in no way be constrictive. If a recipe calls for chicken eggs, but all you have are a couple of thrush eggs, use those without fear. Similarly, a single kwama egg is roughly equivalent to about four good-sized chicken eggs. If you have been cursed with the inability to eat wheat by some malicious rogue mage, an all-purpose gluten-free flour substitute can be used in most of the recipes in this collection. For a more comprehensive list of dietary qualifications, see the list in the appendix.

If certain herbs are unavailable where you are, simple substitutions can be easily made. Sage, for example, is a very good stand-in for elves ear, and cranberries provide much the same color and tart flavor as true snowberries. These substitutions will not provide you with the various physical and magical buffs as their original counterparts would, but they will nonetheless give you an approximation of the flavors of Tamriel.

While mushrooms are plentiful throughout Tamriel, it's vital that you know which types are safe to eat. I once knew an intrepid Dunmer who set out to create recipes for all the mushrooms species that exist. He was unsuccessful. As a wise man once quipped, "All mushrooms are edible at least once . . ." I can't advise that you go taking bites out of mushrooms at random to see what's safe, though. In the meantime, a common button mushroom will serve until you become an expert on Tamriel's numerous mushroom varieties and their assorted side effects.

When it comes to meats, there are a few ways to go: You can smoke it, salt it, cook it, preserve it with ice wraith teeth, or eat it raw. The Bosmer wood elves are particularly known for their meat-heavy diet, making a meal of just about anything that crosses their path—and I mean anything. For those with a more

discerning palate, there are thankfully many delicious options roaming the wilds of Tamriel. Venison, mammoth, goat, rabbit, the elusive pheasant, and even the little domestic chicken—provided it doesn't belong to someone else—are all delectable. In a pinch, even cave bear can be roasted up over a campfire, but I hear it can be a little greasy. Similarly, the rivers and coastlines are teeming with edibles just waiting to be caught: salmon, Nordic barnacles, pearl oysters, clams, slaughterfish, and many more.

Some say only a Nord can work the soil in Skyrim, but many other races have also made a home in the chilliest region of Tamriel. Using a combination of ingenuity and sheer stubbornness, they have adapted some of the favorite recipes from their homelands to suit the ingredients of Skyrim. None are more able to adapt than the Khajiit, who are a roving people by nature, and often carry with them a wild assortment of spices and seasonings. A meal by their campfires is an opportunity not to be missed.

In short, the foods of Tamriel are what you make them. Hopefully this modest collection of recipes will give you a good starting point for your own edible experiments over the hearthfire.

Watch the skies, traveler. I wish you good eating.

— CHELSEA MONROE-CASSEL

THE TASTES OF TAMRIEL

The cuisine of Tamriel is as varied as the races that inhabit its distinctive regions. Each dish reflects the culture, geography, and economic realities that have shaped the peoples who created it. Add to that a dash of history here, plus a pinch of ancestral pride there, and you'll find a rich and flavorful array of recipes to delight the senses.

NORDS

Nord cuisine reflects the harsh climate and rugged landscape that has shaped their warrior culture. Where farming is difficult, wild game supplies a significant portion of the local diet. These meats can be preserved through smoking, drying, pickling, or salting. A good deal of fish also features, such as salmon caught in the quick-flowing White River. Among the most mouth-watering Nord foods, however, are those served at great feasts. Large roasts of mammoth, horker, and assorted game meats are cooked over a spit in the center of the hall, while rustic desserts made with juniper or snowberries are cooked in cob ovens. Those same northern ingredients make their way into Nord mead, which has developed a reputation for its strength in other parts of Tamriel.

REDGUARD

Redguard residents hold to the belief that the estrangement between two of their deities causes difficulties for growing food, but it is just as likely that the Alik'r Desert is to blame. What arable land exists on the plains surrounding Hammerfell is used to grow drought-hardy crops and graze domesticated livestock such as goats. These foods are often dehydrated or salted for storage and trade, but everyday meals are usually cooked by methods designed to beat the heat: Flatbreads are baked in seconds on searing-hot stones rather than in ovens, and hearty stews are set over coals to cook over long periods of time. Fortunately, trade from the port cities brings much needed variety to Redguard larders, and the fiery peppers grown in Hammerfell are much prized by cooks in other regions.

BOSMER

The wood elves of Tamriel, the **Bosmer**, made a pact long ago with Y'ffre, their forest deity. In this Green Pact, they swore to abstain from eating or harming any plant from their native Valenwood, which has resulted in a heavily meat-based diet. Their skilled hunters return from patrols with venison, rabbit, and other game meats, as well as foraged eggs from nests high in the treetops. Cooking is something of an afterthought, or reserved for meat served to guests. Some game meat is preserved by drying or salting, but in general the Bosmer hunt and forage as needed.

KHAJIIT

Known for their insatiable sweet tooth, the **Khajiit** enjoy a wide array of specialty dishes and desserts, many of which are cooked over the fires of the camps they set up during their travels. The famous black market substance known as moonsugar is a key ingredient in a majority of Khajiit cooking, and as a result they have developed a tolerance to amounts of the stuff that would lay other races low. This affection for moonsugar has limited the amount of trade that many merchants are willing to take on with the Khajiit, which in turn limits the variety of ingredients they are able to incorporate into their cooking (at least, legally obtained ingredients). They always have wares for those with the coin, including skooma and sweetrolls of questionable origin.

IMPERIALS

Imperial cooks approach food the same way they face the rest of life: in a straightforward and proud manner. As shrewd diplomats and traders, they stock their larders with many of the best ingredients Tamriel has to offer. Cyrodiil's central location in Tamriel, paired with its wealth and power, assures that the Imperials eat well from a variety of meats, vegetables, and spices from across the continent.

ORSIMER

The **Orsimer** are a strong and fiercely loyal race. Although many also live in their capital city Orsinium, most live in strongholds scattered across Tamriel. Each such stronghold must be self-sufficient, so the Orsimers' diet is predominantly made up of practical foods that can be easily grown, foraged, hunted, and stored. There is little room for frills, but they do appreciate a variety of spices and seasonings when trade brings them their way. Because they are such tight-knit communities, Orismer often prepare large communal meals that are shared among all members of the stronghold, often using their forge fires to roast skewers of meat.

ALTMER

Mostly isolated as they are on their Summerset Isles, the **Altmer** have had ample time to perfect their cuisine without the interference of outside races. However, with the relatively new opening of their shores to outsiders, they have begun to embrace the best culinary innovations of Tamriel's other residents. A race that values beauty and perfection, they harbor very strict rules regarding table manners and deportment. Nonetheless, they enjoy a wide array of haute cuisine, dining on the most daintily crafted sweets washed down with fine liqueurs and brandies.

BRETONS

Bretons are known for their exceptional skill with spells, and in truth, their skills in the kitchen are no less magical. They enjoy a prosperous trade up and down the Iliac Bay, and the soil of High Rock provides fertile ground for numerous crops. However, the rigid economic hierarchy of Breton culture is also reflected in their cuisine: Professional cooks prepare the most elaborate and expensive dishes for the aristocracy, while the impoverished peasantry must make do with what they can grow or forage themselves.

DUNMER

Dunmer, Tamriel's dark elves, inhabit a part of the land that is almost entirely unsuited to agriculture. Morrowind's dark volcanic terrain makes farming or hunting very difficult. Despite this hardship, the Dunmer have learned over the ages to live in harmony with the inhospitable landscape: They gather kwama eggs, cultivate crops of ash yams, and maintain herds of domesticated guar, from which they harvest meat and hides. A wide variety of drinks also feature in Dunmer cuisine, made from saltrice and native fruits.

ARGONIANS

Argonian cuisine is perhaps the most impenetrable for outsiders. The Black Marsh is considered by most to be a dismal place, but the Argonians' superb swimming skills make them a perfect fit for the region. Composed largely of raw fish and swamp plants collected throughout the marshes, Argonian dishes are for only the bravest of other races. Often eaten raw, albeit seasoned with exotic spices and rich sauces, the fish and small creatures Argonians harvest in nets and traps sustain them in a way that is wholly unique in Tamriel.

CELEBRATIONS

No matter their race or region, the residents of Tamriel love their festivals. Some celebrations, like the Redguard Koomu Alezer'i in Sentinel have been held for thousands of years, while some are more recent additions to the calendar. Generally, however, they all have in common a joyful atmosphere and plenty of food and drink.

Both the Old Life and the New Life Festivals are fêtes that span all of Tamriel. At their core, these joyous events celebrate life and the rebirth of the sun after the darkest day of the year. The holidays are recognized in different ways by the various races, often with games or various physical challenges and a good deal of food and drink.

Many Nords, for example, choose to jump into frozen lakes before warming themselves by a fire with a flagon of mead, while the Khajiit set themselves a variety of larcenous objectives with a toast of **Skooma** (page 173) as a reward. **San's Spiced Wine** (page 171) and homemade **Sweet Nog** (page 179) are popular gifts, best enjoyed alongside sweets such as **Spiced Root Cake** (page 155) or **Birch Cookies** (page 137).

Heart's Day is a popular holiday amongst Tamriel's lovers, and a day on which rooms are free in taverns and inns across the continent. Couples can share a steaming pot of **Elsweyr Fondue** (page 117) in a darkened tavern corner. Khajiit like to show their affection with a stolen **Sweetroll** (page 157), and even the normally taciturn Mer have been known to share a slender bottle of **Snowberry Cordial** (page 175) with a loved one.

Celebrations for First Planting and the beginning of spring include recipes utilizing the flowers of the field and the honey from the bees newly woken from their winter slumber. Old grudges are abandoned over slices of aromatic **Lavender and Honey Bread** (page 87), which pairs beautifully with fresh butter and a flagon of **Honningbrew Mead** (page 162). The sweetness of flowers can also be enjoyed with crisp bites of **Honeycomb Brittle** (page 139) and smooth **Honey Pudding** (page 143).

Fishing Day is a Breton holiday that has been gaining popularity across Skyrim as well as other parts of Tamriel where fishing has been not only a livelihood but a way of life for many generations. Nets and hooks are laid aside in favor of bowls of **Coastal Clam Chowder** (page 93) and savory **Rye Crisps** (page 85). **Seared Nordic Barnacles** (page 107) are enjoyed with a reserve bottle of spiced **Nord Mead** (page 165). Larger families also enjoy a **Horker Loaf** (page 131) with all the trimmings.

Harvest's End is a time of celebrating the bounty of the year's harvest and a well-deserved reward for a season of hard work in field and orchard. **Goatherd's Pie** (page 121) is commonly found on feast tables piled high with fruits, vegetables, and roast meats, while over large fires bubbling cauldrons of **Vegetable Soup** (page 101) simmer away. The taverns offer free drinks throughout the day, including measures of the local recipe for **Water of Life** (page 185).

A COOK'S GUIDE TO HOMESTEADING

When it comes to successful cooking, one often need look no further than high-quality, fresh ingredients. And if you are lucky enough to own your own homestead, the ingredients are the freshest available, grown in your very own garden. Whether you are a renowned upstanding citizen or a quietly disreputable thief, there's a house in Tamriel that is perfect for your needs. If not, you can always build your own! The satisfaction of living in a home that you've labored over isn't too different from the extra flavor in a dish you've cooked yourself. And a perk of finding that perfect plot of land is that you can customize it to your own needs and desires.

A fully stocked kitchen is every cook's dream, complete with oven, butter churn, roasting spit, cool cellar storage, and plenty of storage and workspace. But the customization doesn't stop there: If you are a brewer or an avid fan of mead, why not install an apiary outside your home to house bees and produce honey? Let's be honest, nobody knows for sure what "secret ingredients" go into the vats in the Black-Briar Meadery, but with your own honey source at home, there's no longer a need to roll the dice on unknown bottles of questionable origin.

If you love to cook, then a greenhouse is a clear choice for one of the wings of your home, especially in colder regions like Skyrim where a hothouse can make all the difference in lengthening the growing season. It will enable you to have a steady source of leeks, tomatoes, potatoes, carrots, gourds, and a wide variety of herbs for both cooking and alchemy.

Be sure to read the *Beginner's Guide to Homesteading* for additional tips and tricks on how to create a manor house that is perfect for you.

Firewatch

Sadrith
Mora

Necrom

urnhold

Tear

Thorn

Archon

BASICS

SPICES, SEASONINGS, & CONDIMENTS

A salt pile is one of the most important ingredients for cooking any recipe in Tamriel. In fact, many chefs swear that you cannot even contemplate cooking something without a few piles of salt in your pantry.

Other seasonings are scarcely less important. They are so integral to the making of a flavorful finished dish that some handed-down recipes don't even include them, with the assumption you simply know to tweak to taste. Spices and seasonings often have a history all their own, and the farther they travel the more costly and difficult they are to obtain. Even the smallest jar of spice is a prized possession in the larders of small villages.

Although every village, and indeed often every family, has its own special blend of seasoning, these are three of the most common mixes found in Tamriel.

NORD SPICES

This warming blend of spices brings to life any cold-weather recipe that includes it. The warmth of the cardamom and cinnamon is balanced by the bite of mace, clove, and grains, making it a solid addition to desserts, baking, and hot drinks.

LEVEL

Cooking: 5 minutes   **Makes:** about 1/8 cup

1½ tablespoons ground cardamom

¾ teaspoon ground cinnamon

¼ teaspoon ground mace

¼ teaspoon ground cloves

⅛ teaspoon ground grains of paradise

1. Mix together all of the ground ingredients, then store in a small airtight jar.

USED IN:

Snowberry Sauce (page 31)

Spiced Butter (page 33)

Stewed Apples and Eidar Cheese (page 63)

Braided Bread (page 71)

Oatmeal Raisin Shortbread (page 145)

Apple Cobbler (page 149)

Snowberry Crostata (page 151)

23

STORMCLOAK SEASONING

This is one of the most popular seasoning mixes across the breadth of Skyrim, where nearly every garden boasts a little corner dedicated to growing most of these ingredients. The grains of paradise are imported, and if the cost is too dear, ordinary black pepper can be substituted. It makes for a mixture that goes well with vegetables, fish, meat, and savory baking.

LEVEL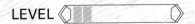

Cooking: 5 minutes **Makes:** about ⅛ cup

2 teaspoons dried dill

½ teaspoon grains of paradise

1 teaspoon mustard powder

2 teaspoons fennel seeds

1. Crush or grind all the ingredients together using a mortar and pestle or a clean spice grinder, then store in a small airtight jar.

USED IN:

Rye Pie Dough (page 39)

Hot Mudcrab Dip (page 59)

Potato Cheddar Soup (page 97)

Vegetable Soup (page 101)

Baked White River Salmon (page 109)

Chicken Dumplings (page 111)

Companions Meatball Bake (page 115)

Festival Hand Pies (page 119)

Horker Loaf (page 131)

IMPERIAL SEASONING

Brought by Imperial troops and their regiment cooks, this mix
has put down roots and is gaining in popularity in Skyrim, even
if the Imperials themselves are not. It's a unique combination of
savory flavors and a bright citrus profile lent by the coriander,
and it is delicious on vegetables and fish.

LEVEL

Cooking: 5 minutes **Makes:** about ⅛ cup

3 teaspoons dried marjoram

3 teaspoons dried savory

1 teaspoon coriander seeds

¼ teaspoon white pepper

1. Crush or grind ingredients together using a mortar and pestle or a
   clean spice grinder, then store in a small airtight jar.

USED IN:

Imperial Mushroom Sauce (page 37)

Mushroom and Vegetable Risotto (page 51)

S'jirra's Famous Potato Bread (page 81)

Coastal Clam Chowder (page 93)

Imperial Mulled Wine (page 167)

CUSTARD SAUCE

A good custard sauce should be thick and creamy, and is equally
delicious poured over desserts as it is eaten straight off the spoon.
The shaggy cows of Skyrim give especially good milk for custard, as
it is rich with the flavors of their mountainside grazing.

LEVEL

Cooking: 10 minutes   **Cooling:** 1 hour
Makes: about 2 cups   **Pairs well with:** Apple Cobbler (page 149)

1½ cups whole milk

2 teaspoons cornstarch

2 tablespoons sugar

2 eggs

Dash of almond extract

1. Combine the milk, cornstarch, sugar, and eggs in a small saucepan
   over medium heat. Whisk continuously while the mixture heats up,
   until the eggs are completely incorporated.

2. Stir occasionally for 6 to 8 minutes, until the custard is thick enough
   to coat the back of a spoon; it should be around 160°F.

3. Remove from the heat and stir in the almond flavoring extract, then
   strain into a clean small pitcher. Cover with plastic and refrigerate to
   cool for about an hour.

USED IN:

Boiled Creme Treat (page 153)

SNOWBERRY SAUCE

A lot of cooking in Tamriel makes use of what ingredients are available, and the snowberry is one of the most common edible plants in the more northern parts of Skyrim. With rich spices and a dash of warming port, this tart sauce pairs beautifully with a variety of meats as well as desserts.

LEVEL

Cooking: 30 minutes total **Makes:** about 2 cups
Pairs well with: Horker Loaf (page 131), ice cream

12 ounces fresh or frozen cranberries, whole

1 cup water

⅔ cup packed brown sugar

½ teaspoon Nord Spices (page 23)

1 to 2 tablespoons port wine (optional)

1. Combine the cranberries, water, brown sugar, and Nord Spices in a medium pot over medium heat. Bring up to a simmer and allow the sauce to cook until the cranberries are soft and bursting.

2. Remove from the heat and mash the berries so you have a relatively even mixture. At this point, you can simply add just enough port, if using, to get a consistency you like, or press the mixture through a sieve for a much finer sauce.

SPICED BUTTER

Ordinary butter is readily available across Tamriel and can be purchased from innkeepers, vendors, and merchants for use in many recipes. However, some special occasions or unusual dishes benefit from something a little extra. This richly flavored butter melds beautifully with roasted vegetables, but is also a wonderful way to start off breakfast.

LEVEL

Prep: 5 minutes **Makes:** ½ cup butter
Pairs well with: Baked Ash Yams (page 45), warm toast, oatmeal

8 tablespoons (1 stick)
   unsalted butter, softened

¼ teaspoon dark molasses

¼ teaspoon Nord Spices
   (page 23)

1. Combine all the ingredients in a small bowl and blend until fully mixed. Cover with plastic and store in the refrigerator.

BRAJDWOOD
INN

RUSTIC MUSTARD

Brightly flavored with a characteristic mustard bite, this spread can be commonly found in small jars tucked up on cellar shelves amid other preserved goods. Its sharp flavor helps brighten meals during the long days of winter.

LEVEL

Prep: 10 minutes **Makes:** about 1 cup **Pairs well with:** ham

5 tablespoons mustard powder

½ cup packed brown sugar

1 teaspoon salt

1 cup heavy cream

1 tablespoon olive oil

2 tablespoons apple cider vinegar

1. Combine the mustard powder, brown sugar, and salt in a small saucepan over medium heat.

2. Add the cream bit by bit, stirring, until it turns into a nice pale mixture with an even consistency. Add the oil and vinegar, then cook for about 5 minutes, or until the mustard has thickened and the color has turned darker. The mustard will keep, covered, for several weeks in the refrigerator.

IMPERIAL MUSHROOM SAUCE

This rustic sauce has its origins in the outlying regions from which the auxiliary soldiers are drawn. What was simple country food has become a favorite staple on the tables of even generals in the Imperial army.

LEVEL

Cooking: 10 minutes **Makes:** about 4 servings
Pairs well with: Horker Loaf (page 131)

2 tablespoons unsalted butter

10 ounces button mushrooms, diced

2 tablespoons all-purpose flour

½ cup chicken broth

Splash of white wine vinegar

1 teaspoon Imperial Seasoning (page 27)

2 tablespoons heavy cream

Salt and pepper

1. Melt the butter in a large saucepan over medium heat, then add the mushrooms, giving them a quick stir to coat in the butter. Let the mushrooms cook for about 5 minutes, or until soft.

2. Toss in the flour, stirring until it is absorbed, then add the chicken broth. Stir and continue to cook for a minute or two, until the mixture thickens somewhat. Stir in the Imperial Seasoning and cream, and season with salt and pepper to taste.

SWEET CROSTATA DOUGH

LEVEL

Prep: 10 minutes **Chilling:** 1 hour
Makes: 1 crostata crust or several smaller tarts

1 cup all-purpose flour

½ cup rye flour

Pinch of salt

2 tablespoons brown sugar

6 tablespoons cold unsalted
butter

2 tablespoons ice water or as
needed

1. Combine the all-purpose flour, rye flour, salt, and brown sugar in a
medium bowl. Rub in the butter with your fingers until you have a
consistency like fine breadcrumbs.

2. Gradually stir in just enough water until the dough comes together.
Form into a disk, wrap with plastic, and refrigerate for at least an
hour before using.

USED IN:

Sheogorath's Strawberry Tarts (page 147)
Snowberry Crostata (page 151)

RYE PIE DOUGH

LEVEL

Prep: 10 minutes **Chilling:** 30 minutes **Makes:** 1 batch

1 cup all-purpose flour

1 cup rye flour

½ teaspoon salt

½ teaspoon Stormcloak
Seasoning (page 25)

6 tablespoons cold unsalted
butter

⅓ cup ice water

1. Combine the all-purpose flour, rye flour, salt, and Stormcloak
Seasoning in a medium bowl. Rub in the butter until you have a
consistency like coarse breadcrumbs.

2. Add just enough water to bring the dough together. Form into a
disk, wrap in plastic, and refrigerate for at least 30 minutes, or until
ready to use.

USED IN:

Leek and Cheese Crostata (page 61)
Chicken Dumplings (page 111)
Festival Hand Pies (page 119)
Kwama Egg Quiche (page 125)

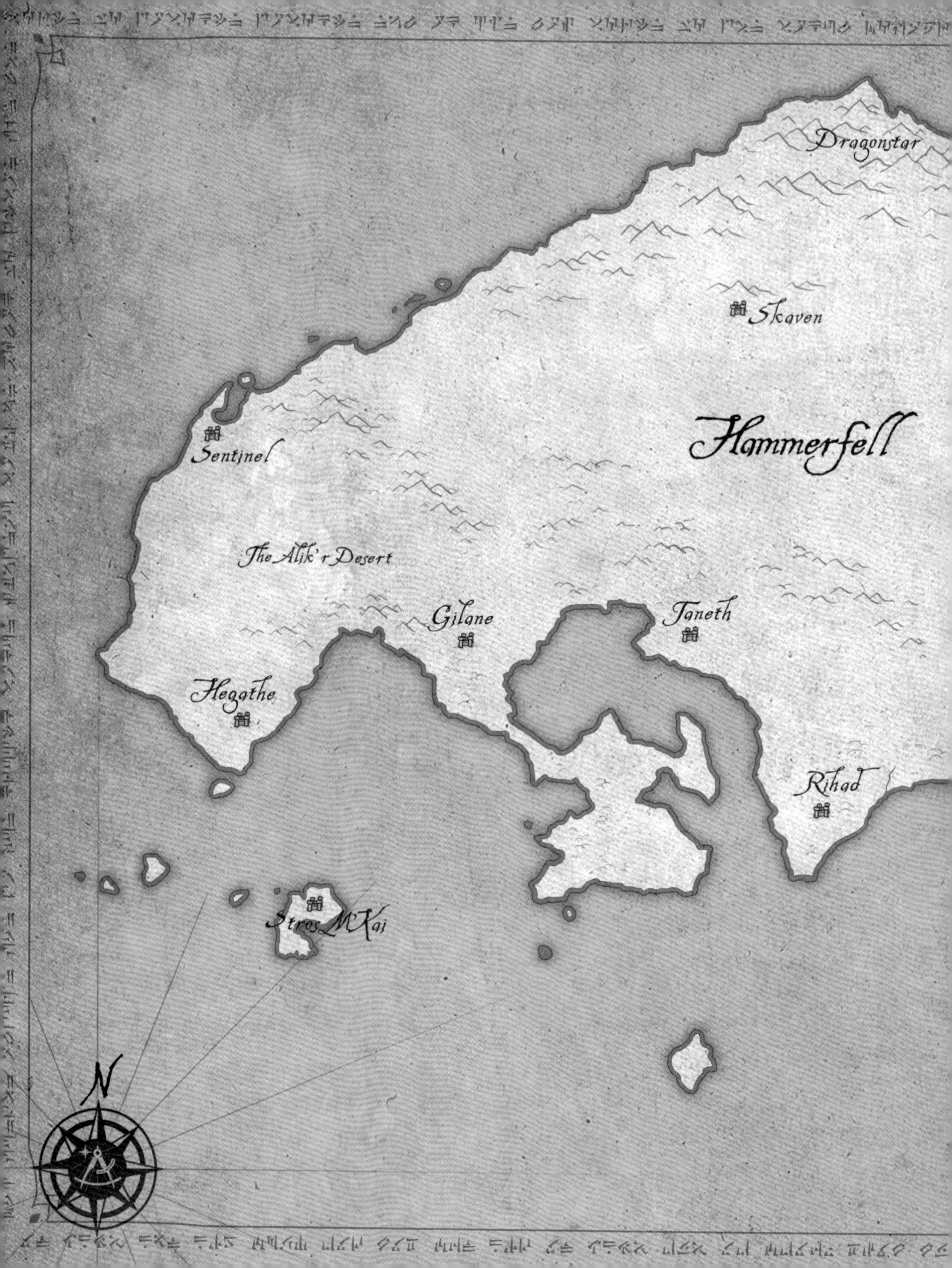

Dragonstar

Skaven

Hammerfell

Sentinel

The Alik'r Desert

Gilane   Taneth

Hegathe

Rihad

Stros M'Kai

N

Blinhir

SIDES, STARTERS, & SNACKS

BABY CARROTS IN MOONSUGAR GLAZE

This dish can often be found cooking over the fires of Khajiit traders in their camps. Like many Khajiit dishes it uses moonsugar, but this particular recipe approximates the flavors of the sugar without any of its addictive side effects—and it's far more legal.

LEVEL

Cooking: 10 minutes **Makes:** 4 servings

Pairs well with: Juniper Lamb Chops (page 129) or other meaty roasts, sweet wine

1 pound baby carrots

1 teaspoon salt

1 tablespoon unsalted butter

¼ cup packed brown sugar

½ teaspoon ground cardamom

Zest of ½ orange

1. Bring a medium-sized saucepan filled with water to a boil. Add the carrots and salt and cook for about 8 minutes, until tender.

2. While the carrots are cooking, melt the butter and sugar in a second medium saucepan over medium heat. Add the cardamom and orange zest, stirring to combine. Keep this mixture on low while the carrots finish cooking.

3. Drain the carrots and add them to the pan with the sugar. Turn the heat back up to medium and stir the carrots to coat for several minutes. This dish can be made ahead of time and easily reheated.

BAKED ASH YAMS

Ash yams are one of the few vegetables that thrives in Morrowind's climate, especially after the volcanic explosion of the Red Mountain. Some of the Dunmer fleeing that devastation thoughtfully packed yams and introduced them to Skyrim, where some Nords have added their own distinct flavors to this recipe.

LEVEL

Prep: 5 minutes **Cooking:** 45 minutes to 1 hour
Makes: 4 servings **Pairs well with:** Spiced Butter (page 33), roasted vegetables

4 large yams

1 recipe Spiced Butter
  (page 33)

¼ cup crumbled goat cheese

Parsley, minced, for
  garnishing

1. Preheat the oven to 425°F. Clean and dry the yams, then prick them all over several times with a knife.

2. Place the yams directly on an oven rack placed in the middle position with a baking sheet on the rack below to catch any drippings. Bake for 45 to 60 minutes, or until you can easily pierce each yam with a knife. Remove from the oven.

3. Wrapping one yam at a time in a kitchen towel, cut a large *X* on the top of each and press on both ends of the yam to open the cuts. Top with as much Spiced Butter as you like, then sprinkle goat cheese and parsley over the top to finish.

GRILLED LEEKS

Although leeks can be a little finicky to grow, it's no wonder they thrive around all the riverlands in Skyrim. This rugged vegetable is popular in stews and savory pies, but it is also delicious in its own right and can often be spied gracing the tables of the rich and poor alike.

LEVEL

Prep: 5 minutes   **Cooking:** 15 minutes
Makes: 4 servings   **Pairs well with:** Baked White River Salmon (page 109)

4 large leeks

2 tablespoons olive oil

2 tablespoons grated
    Parmesan cheese

Salt and pepper

1. Begin by cutting off the tough dark green tops of the leeks, leaving the more tender white and paler green sections. Don't cut off the root end, which will help the leeks stay together while cooking. Slice each leek in half and rinse thoroughly to remove any dirt.

2. Bring a large pot of water to a boil over high heat and drop the leeks in, letting them cook until they begin to soften, about 5 minutes. Remove from the pot and place in a bowl of ice water to stop them from continuing to cook and also hold the color.

3. In a wide frying pan, heat the olive oil over medium-high heat. Place the leeks cut-side down in the pan and cook for several minutes until they are starting to brown. Transfer to a serving plate, sprinkle with Parmesan cheese, and season with salt and pepper to taste.

BOSMER BITES

Because of their adherence to the Green Pact, the Bosmer are severely limited in their diet. Forbidden to harm plants in their native Valenwood forest, they rely on deadfall and peat to fuel their sparse fires and eat mostly meat that is either cured or quickly cooked. Fruits are only allowed if they have already fallen from the tree, and the seeds must be replanted, lest they face the wrath of an irate forest. This basic recipe works very well with a variety of tree fruits and assorted meats. The Bosmer use whatever freshly cured meat they have on hand, no matter the dubious origin.

LEVEL

Prep: 5 minutes **Cook time:** 30 minutes
Makes: 16 pieces **Pairs well with:** nuts, dried fruits

2 cups balsamic vinegar

½ cup granulated sugar

Pinch of salt

About 2 ounces Brie cheese, softened

2 peaches, pitted and sliced into 8 pieces each

¼ pound sliced prosciutto

1. Begin by making a balsamic glaze. Pour the balsamic vinegar, sugar, and a pinch of salt into a medium saucepan over medium-high heat. Bring the vinegar to a boil, stirring to combine. Reduce the heat to medium and continue to simmer until the sauce has reduced by half, about 20 minutes. Set aside to cool completely.

2. To assemble the bites, cut a dollop of cheese, a little more than a teaspoon, and spread it over a slice of peach. Wrap a piece of prosciutto around the cheese and peach, then thread onto a small skewer.

3. Drizzle with the balsamic glaze to serve.

TIP

Feel free to experiment with other flavors by swapping out the peaches and Brie with other fruits and cheeses. Other suggested pairings include:
› Apple and sharp cheddar
› Cantaloupe and burrata
› Fig and blue cheese

MUSHROOM AND VEGETABLE RISOTTO

Versions of this dish can be found all across Tamriel, but using four types of Balmoran mushrooms can give this dish a special regional flavor. This dish is also popular in Skyrim, where its stick-to-the-rib quality makes it a common dish from farmer's cottage to Jarl's hall. After all, in a land of perpetual winter, everybody needs a bowl of warm comfort food from time to time.

LEVEL

Prep: 15 minutes   **Cooking:** 40 minutes
Makes: 4 to 6 servings   **Pairs well with:** Baked White River Salmon (page 109)

¼ cup (½ stick) unsalted butter

2 cloves garlic, minced

1 leek, white and pale green parts chopped

1 small carrot, diced

8 ounces mixed mushrooms, roughly chopped

4 cups vegetable stock

1½ cups arborio rice

½ teaspoon Imperial Seasoning (page 27)

½ cup grated Parmesan cheese

Salt and pepper

1. Melt the butter in a large sauté pan over medium heat, then add the garlic and leek. Cook for a few minutes until soft and fragrant. Add the carrot and mushrooms, stirring to incorporate and make sure everything is covered in butter. Add a splash of the vegetable stock, then cover the pan and let cook for about 5 minutes, until the carrots are beginning to soften.

2. Add the rice and Imperial Seasoning, and stir for a minute or so. Begin gradually pouring in a little of the broth at a time, waiting until each batch has been absorbed before adding in more.

3. When just about all the liquid has been absorbed, stir in the Parmesan cheese. Season to taste with salt and pepper. The final consistency should be thick but not stuck together, so add a little more water or broth if need be to loosen it up.

> **TIP**
>
> Feel free to experiment with various mushroom types, but cremini, button, porcini, and portobello mushrooms are a great place to start.

DOUBLE-BAKED POTATOES

The humble potato is one of Skyrim's staple ingredients, found growing on every farm. Like many fruits and vegetables, potatoes store surprisingly well in barrels. While considered more practical than valuable and not good for much more than eating, this recipe makes them taste like they're worth their weight in Septims.

LEVEL

Prep: 15 minutes **Cooking:** 2 hours
Makes: 4 servings **Pairs well with:** Juniper Lamb Chops (page 129), Horker Loaf (page 131)

2 baking potatoes

5 tablespoons salted butter, divided

¼ cup whole milk or heavy cream

¼ cup shredded cheddar cheese

Pinch of salt

1. Preheat the oven to 400°F. Clean and dry the potatoes, then pierce several times to allow steam to escape, and lightly coat with 1 tablespoon of the butter for a crispier skin. Place directly on an oven rack in the middle position with a baking sheet on the rack below to catch any drippings and bake for about 1 hour, or until they are soft all the way through when poked with a knife.

2. When the potatoes are done, cut each in half lengthwise and gently scoop the insides into a bowl, leaving the skins intact. Add the remaining 4 tablespoons of butter and the milk or cream, cheddar cheese, and salt, mashing as you would for mashed potatoes. Scoop this filling back into the potato skins.

3. Turn the oven down to 375°F and arrange the filled potato halves on a baking sheet. Put the potatoes back in the oven and cook for about 15 minutes, or until they have started to brown on top. If you'd like a more dramatic color, put the tray of potatoes under the broiler for a minute or so, just to brown the tops a bit more.

> **TIP**
>
> This is a very simple recipe with good results, but for an extra treat, mix in some crumbled bacon with the filling before you put it back into the skins. Some Imperial or Stormcloak Seasoning can also give a nice boost of flavor.

REDGUARD RICE

Redolent with rich spices, this dish is prepared in a single pot, making it a great candidate for cooking on the road. It is, at its heart, a very traditional Redguard recipe, although it can be easily tweaked and improved based on locally available ingredients.

LEVEL

Prep: 5 minutes **Cooking:** at least 30 minutes **Makes:** 4 servings
Pairs well with: Nord Mead (page 165), Imperial Mushroom Sauce (page 37)

2 tablespoons unsalted butter

½ onion, minced

1 pound ground lamb

½ teaspoon ground
   cinnamon

½ teaspoon hot paprika

½ teaspoon whole coriander
   seeds

1 tablespoon molasses

1 cup wild rice

2 cups chicken broth

Chopped parsley for
   garnishing

1. Melt the butter in a medium saucepan over medium heat and cook the onion for several minutes, until soft and brown. Add the ground lamb and stir until the meat is completely browned, about 8 to 10 minutes.

2. Stir in the cinnamon, paprika, coriander, and molasses, then the wild rice. Pour in the chicken broth, cover, and simmer for 35 to 45 minutes, until most of the liquid has been absorbed and the rice is soft.

3. Uncover and continue to cook, stirring occasionally, until the whole mixture is fairly dry. Remove from the heat and stir in the parsley before serving.

ARGONIAN SWAMP SHRIMP BOIL

While not much from the Argonian kitchen is palatable to other races, a few dishes have proven wildly popular even with the Altmer, although you'd be hard pressed to get them to admit as much. The Argonians prefer to make this recipe using swamp shrimp from the Black Marshes, but in a pinch, the northern varieties of prawn caught off the coast of Skyrim will do.

LEVEL

Cooking: 10 minutes **Makes:** 8 small servings or enough for a gathering
Pairs well with: roasted corn on the cob, sweet white wine

2 cups water

1 pound shrimp, deveined

½ cup soy sauce

1 tablespoon cornstarch

1 tablespoon brown sugar

2 tablespoons molasses

½ teaspoon dried thyme

½ teaspoon chili powder

1 tablespoon unsalted butter

2 tablespoons cream

1. In a large saucepan over medium heat, bring the water to a boil and add the shrimp. Boil for about 2 to 3 minutes, until they are a nice bright pink. Scoop the cooked shrimp out and set aside; if you'd like, remove the tails at this point.

2. In a small bowl, stir together the soy sauce and cornstarch until the latter is completely dissolved. Add this to the boiling water along with the brown sugar, molasses, thyme, and chili powder.

3. Stir for several minutes until the whole mixture has reduced somewhat and is a nice thick consistency, but still pourable. Remove from the heat and stir in the butter and cream. Transfer the shrimp to a serving dish and either pour the sauce over them or serve it on the side for dipping.

HOT MUDCRAB DIP

Let's face it—we've all been chased around by those pesky oversized crabs. Now you can take your revenge on those self-important crustaceans by mixing them into this tasty dip. They bring friends, so why shouldn't you feed them to yours?

LEVEL

Prep: 5 minutes   **Cooking:** 20 minutes

Makes: 1 party-size serving (roughly 8 to 10 people)   **Pairs well with:** crackers, sliced baguette

8 ounces softened cream cheese

¼ cup heavy cream

Splash of white wine vinegar

8 ounces crab meat, shredded

1 teaspoon Stormcloak Seasoning (page 25)

½ cup shredded cheddar cheese

2 tablespoons minced chives

Pinch of chili powder

3 tablespoons grated Parmesan cheese

Crackers or baguette slices for serving

1. Preheat the oven to 400°F.

2. Beat together the cream cheese and heavy cream in a medium bowl. Add the remaining ingredients except the Parmesan, stirring until it is evenly blended.

3. Transfer the mixture to a medium the baking dish and smooth out the top. Sprinkle with the Parmesan cheese and bake for about 20 minutes, or until the dip is hot and the cheese is starting to turn golden brown on top. Serve with crackers or a sliced baguette.

LEEK AND CHEESE CROSTATA

Combining two of Skyrim's more common ingredients, the result is a hearty tart that is great for picnics and afternoon snacks, but can also easily be served as a side dish next to a main course. It is popularly made with either eidar cheese or goat cheese, but a good cheddar also works well.

LEVEL

Prep: 25 minutes **Cooking:** 25 minutes
Makes: 1 tart (6 to 8 servings) **Pairs well with:** beer, Potage le Magnifique (page 103)

1 recipe Rye Pie Dough (page 39)

2 large leeks, white and pale green parts, thinly sliced

2 tablespoons unsalted butter

1 tablespoon all-purpose flour

⅓ to ½ cup heavy cream

1 cup shredded cheddar or Gruyère cheese

1 tablespoon grated Parmesan cheese for topping

Salt and pepper

1. Preheat the oven to 350°F and line a baking sheet with parchment paper. Roll out the pie dough on a lightly floured surface to about ⅛ inch thick. Try to keep a roughly round shape, but uneven edges are fine. Carefully drape this over the prepared baking sheet and set aside.

2. Melt the butter in a medium skillet over medium heat. Add the leeks and cook for about 5 to 10 minutes, until they are soft and just starting to turn golden brown. Add the flour and stir until incorporated. Pour the cream in a little at a time, stirring until it has all been mostly absorbed and the mixture has thickened.

3. Remove from the heat and stir in the cheddar or Gruyère cheese, and season with salt and pepper to taste. Let this mixture cool for about 10 minutes, then gently transfer it to the middle of the prepared dough. Spread the filling out until only about 1½ inches around the edges of the crust have been left bare. Sprinkle the filling with Parmesan, then gently fold the bare edge of the crust over the filling, overlapping as you go.

4. Bake 25 minutes, or until the top of the filling is starting to turn golden. Allow to cool for a few minutes before slicing and serving.

STEWED APPLES AND EIDAR CHEESE

Try this recipe alongside a hearty slice of meat after a long and arduous quest—you won't be disappointed. Most apples work well in this recipe, but be sure to avoid any poisoned ones by eschewing any apples you find sitting alone on a table with no other food present. As a bonus, this versatile side dish can also do double duty as a dessert. If you're not a fan of eidar cheese's distinct ripeness, try a milder goat cheese crumble or leave it off altogether for a sweeter version.

LEVEL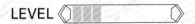

Prep: 10 minutes   **Cooking:** 10 minutes
Makes: 4 small servings   **Pairs well with:** pork dishes, oatmeal

3 tablespoons unsalted butter

4 or 5 large sweet apples, peeled, cored, and diced

¼ cup dried currants

½ cup packed brown sugar

1 teaspoon Nord Spices (page 23)

Pinch of salt

Dash of vanilla extract

2 teaspoons cornstarch

¼ cup cold water

¼ cup crumbled blue cheese for topping

1. Melt the butter in a large sauté pan or skillet over medium heat. Add the apples and cook, stirring occasionally, for about 6 minutes, or until the apples are somewhat tender. Stir in the currants, brown sugar, Nord Spices, salt, and vanilla.

2. In a small bowl, mix together the cornstarch and water, then add to the pan with the apples. Cook another minute or so, until the whole mixture has thickened somewhat. Spoon into serving dishes and top with crumbled blue cheese to taste.

SALTRICE PORRIDGE

The bustling export business of saltrice out of Morrowind
has made this traditional Dunmer dish a popular staple. In
some regions, it has outstripped other breakfast standbys such
as oatmeal, as those grains cannot be cultivated in the short
growing seasons of the northern holds.

LEVEL

Prep: 5 minutes **Cooking:** 45 minutes
Makes: 4 servings **Pairs well with:** Sweetrolls (page 157), a strong breakfast tea

¾ cup white rice

1½ cups water

2½ cups milk

1 to 2 tablespoons honey

Pinch of salt

2 teaspoons vanilla extract

Toppings such as butter,
dried fruits, nuts, ground
cinnamon, ground
nutmeg, or heavy cream

1. Combine the rice and water in a medium saucepan and bring
the water to just under a boil. Lower the temperature to a slow
simmer and cover. Let the rice cook for 10 to 15 minutes, or until
the water is gone.

2. Turn the heat down to low and add the milk slowly in several
batches, about a ½ cup at a time, stirring regularly. Continue
adding milk every 5 minutes or so, until the whole mixture has
thickened to a consistency you like and the rice is soft. Stir in the
honey, salt, and vanilla.

3. Taste and adjust the sweetness to your liking, and serve topped
with your choice of extra honey, butter, dried fruits, nuts,
cinnamon, nutmeg, or heavy cream.

SUNLIGHT SOUFFLÉ

The Gourmet is known for the finicky instructions he provides in *Uncommon Taste*, but this Breton dish is actually simple enough to make, even if you don't have a hickory wood spoon. The result is a light, fluffy meal of egg and cheese with an exquisite flavor that can easily be tweaked and embellished to your own tastes.

LEVEL

Prep: 20 minutes **Cooking:** 20 minutes
Makes: 4 servings **Pairs well with:** fresh fruit, toast, coffee or tea

4 eggs, separated into yolks and whites

2 tablespoons unsalted butter

2 tablespoons all-purpose flour

¾ cup warm milk

2½ ounces grated Parmesan cheese (about ¾ cups)

½ teaspoon nutmeg

Salt and pepper

1. Preheat the oven to 375°F and lightly butter four 6-inch ramekins.

2. In a medium bowl, beat the egg whites until they form soft peaks, then set aside.

3. In a small sauté pan or skillet, melt the butter over medium heat, then stir in the flour to make a roux. Cook for a minute or so, until all of the flour is incorporated, then gradually add in the milk while stirring. Stir for a few more minutes until the whole mixture has thickened. Remove from heat and stir in the cheese, nutmeg, and a dash each of salt and pepper.

4. In a large bowl, beat the egg yolks for about 1 minute, until they are pale and creamy. While still beating, gradually add the cheesy roux from the sauté pan and mix thoroughly. Gently fold in the egg whites, then divide the mixture evenly between the prepared ramekins.

5. Bake for 20 to 25 minutes, or until puffed and light brown on top. Don't be tempted to open the oven door for a peek! It can cause the soufflés to collapse. Serve immediately and behold, the brilliance of the sun!

Dagon Fel

Blacklight

Firewatch

Vvardenfell

Gnisis

Ald'ruhn

Sadrith Mora

Balmora

Seyda Neen

Vivec

Morrowind

Mournhold

N

Narsis

Tear

BAKED GOODS

ecrom

BRAIDED BREAD

Some recipes in Skyrim, like this one, are reserved for special occasions.
This beautiful bread is made in the heart of midwinter, when stores are
running low and better weather seems a long way off. It makes use of some
preciously guarded ingredients with the inclusion of dried fruit, nuts, and
spices. All in all, it makes a special loaf that promises better days to come,
while celebrating the harvest of the previous year.

LEVEL

Prep: 15 minutes   **Rising:** 2 hours   **Baking:** 25 minutes
Makes: 1 loaf   **Pairs well with:** fresh butter and jam

1 cup warm milk

¼ cup packed brown sugar

2 tablespoons melted
    unsalted butter

2 teaspoons instant dry yeast

1 teaspoon Nord Spices
    (page 23)

2 eggs, divided

½ cup mixed nuts and dried
    fruit such as walnuts,
    pecans, dried apricots,
    and dates

3 cups whole wheat flour

2 cups all-purpose flour

1. Combine the milk, brown sugar, butter, yeast, Nord spice, and 1 of
   the eggs in a medium bowl. Stir in the nuts and dried fruit, then mix
   in the flour. Stir to combine the ingredients until they come together
   into a nice dough that is not too sticky.

2. Turn the dough out onto a lightly floured work surface and knead
   for several minutes, until it bounces back when poked. Cover with a
   damp cloth and put in a warm place to rise for about 1 hour, or until
   doubled in size.

3. Preheat the oven to 450°F and grease a baking sheet with butter or
   cover with parchment paper. Divide the dough into 3 equal sections
   and roll them between your hands or on a work surface to create
   ropes about 14 inches long. Pinch one end of the ropes together, then
   place on the baking sheet. Braid the ropes into a fairly tight braid,
   then cover again with a cloth to allow to double in size, about an hour.

4. Beat the remaining egg in a small bowl and brush it onto the dough.
   Bake for about 25 minutes, until the bread is a dark and glossy. Let the
   loaf cool for at least 15 minutes before slicing into it.

MEADOW RYE BREAD

This easy bread makes a flavorful accompaniment to any soup but is especially good with creamy varieties. These loaves can commonly be found in tavern kitchens, where their quick baking time means more satisfied customers.

LEVEL

Prep: 10 minutes   **Baking:** 30 minutes
Makes: 1 loaf   **Pairs well with:** Coastal Clam Chowder (page 93), butter and jam

1 cup whole wheat flour

1½ cups rye flour

¼ cup packed brown sugar

1 tablespoon baking soda

1 teaspoon salt

½ cup dried currants

½ cup stout beer

½ cup buttermilk

1. Preheat the oven to 400°F.

2. In a medium bowl, combine the whole wheat flour, rye flour, brown sugar, baking soda, salt, and currants. Add the beer, then gradually mix in the buttermilk until you have a dough that is not too sticky to handle. Turn out onto a lightly floured surface and knead a few times to make sure everything is evenly distributed.

3. Form into a large rounded oblong loaf and transfer to a baking sheet. Score the top of the dough in a decorative pattern, then bake for about 40 minutes; the bread should sound hollow when tapped on the bottom.

CHEESE SCONES

While scones are often considered a breakfast item, their versatility makes them prime candidates for meals later in the day, especially when given a slightly more savory touch. Feel free to try this recipe with different types of cheese. Eidar and mammoth cheeses are popular in Skyrim, while more adventurous folk can experiment with scuttle from Morrowind made from the flesh of local beetles but similar to cheese. These flaky treats are delicious still warm from the oven and dripping with fresh butter.

LEVEL

Prep: 5 minutes   **Baking:** 15 minutes

Makes: about a dozen   **Pairs well with:** fresh butter, Pea Soup (page 99)

2 cups all-purpose flour

2 tablespoons sugar

2 teaspoons baking powder

½ teaspoon mustard powder

½ teaspoon salt

¼ cup (½ stick) cold unsalted butter, cubed

½ cup sour cream

1 cup shredded aged cheddar cheese

¾ cup buttermilk

1 egg, lightly beaten

2 tablespoons grated Parmesan cheese

1. Preheat the oven to 400°F. In a large bowl, combine the flour, sugar, baking powder, mustard powder, and salt. Rub in the butter with your fingers until you have a fine, crumbly texture.

2. Add the sour cream, stirring until it has been evenly distributed. Mix in the cheese, then add a little buttermilk at a time until you get a good dough with a consistency that isn't too dry or too wet.

3. Lightly flour a work surface and turn out the dough. Press the dough flat and fold it over onto itself a few times to give the scones some layers, then press out to about ½ inch thick in a roughly circular shape. Using a sharp knife, slice the dough into irregular triangles and place them on a baking sheet that has been greased with butter or lined with parchment.

4. Brush the scones with beaten egg and sprinkle with Parmesan cheese, then bake for 15 minutes, or until golden and baked through.

GARLIC BREAD

Nothing pairs with a nice hearty soup quite like a slice or two of thick bread topped with butter and garlic. This easy and quick recipe makes enough for surprise guests or a whole family, and as an added bonus, garlic is good for your health, stamina, and magicka.

LEVEL

Prep: 5 minutes   **Cooking:** 15 minutes
Makes: at least 8 servings   **Pairs well with:** Vegetable Soup (page 101), pasta dishes

1 (16-ounce) loaf Italian bread

½ cup (1 stick) salted butter, softened

3 cloves garlic, minced

1 tablespoon fresh parsley, chopped fine

¼ cup grated Parmesan cheese

1. Preheat the oven to 350°F and set out a large baking sheet. Slice the loaf of bread into pieces about 1 inch thick and place these on the baking sheet. In a small bowl, combine the butter, garlic, and parsley. For a stronger flavor, let the butter and garlic sit together for a few hours before spreading.

2. Spread the mixture evenly onto each slice of bread, then bake for about 10 minutes, or until the butter has soaked into the bread.

3. Remove from the oven and turn on the broiler. Sprinkle the Parmesan cheese on top of each slice, then place under the broiler for a few minutes, until the cheese is melted and slightly golden. Serve right away.

CABBAGE BISCUITS

Although Balmora has since been destroyed, many Dunmer remember the good
eating that could be enjoyed when visiting House Hlaalu's stronghold. These
delicious biscuits make the best of Morrowind ingredients such as scrib cabbage.
Heavily textured, but lightly flavored, they are a great base for a variety of toppings
or as an accompaniment to a hearty soup.

LEVEL

Prep: 30 minutes **Rising:** 1½ hours **Baking:** 20 minutes
Makes: about 16 biscuits **Pairs well with:** sour cream, Pea Soup (page 99)

½ small green cabbage
   (about 1 pound)

2 teaspoons coarse salt

1 tablespoon vegetable oil

Pinch of black pepper

¼ cup (½ stick) salted butter

½ cup whole milk

2 teaspoons granulated
   sugar

1 teaspoon instant dry yeast

2½ cups all-purpose flour
   or more as needed

1 egg

1 tablespoon heavy cream

1. Finely shred the cabbage using a food processor or a grater. Toss the
   cabbage with the coarse salt and let sit in a strainer over a large bowl
   for 30 minutes to 1 hour to drain. Afterward, squeeze the cabbage to
   extract even more water, then discard the excess liquid.

2. Heat the vegetable oil over medium heat in a medium sauté pan or
   skillet, then gently cook the shredded cabbage with the black pepper
   until slightly browned, about 10 to 15 minutes.

3. Transfer the cabbage to a medium bowl, stir in the butter until it's
   melted, then pour the milk over. Add the sugar, then the yeast,
   followed by the egg, then stir together. Gradually mix in enough flour
   until you have a nice dough that pulls away from the sides of the bowl.

4. Knead for several minutes, until the dough bounces back when poked,
   then cover with a towel and place in a warm spot to rise for about 1
   hour, until the dough has risen by at least half.

5. Preheat the oven to 350°F. Roll the dough out to roughly ¾ inch thick,
   then score it in a checkered pattern with a sharp knife. Cut into rounds
   that are roughly 2 to 3 inches across and place on the baking sheet.
   Allow the biscuits to rise again, this time for about 20 minutes. Brush
   the tops with heavy cream, then bake for about 20 minutes, until the
   tops are a golden brown. Best enjoyed the same day.

S'JIRRA'S FAMOUS POTATO BREAD

The strange Khajiit S'jirra is the only one that sells her Famous Potato Bread to those who encounter her at the Faregyl Inn. But because wheat is in such high demand in Skyrim, many Nords have adopted this recipe that adds potato to stretch out the supply of flour. This results in a light flatbread that is delicious fresh from the oven and slathered with butter.

LEVEL

Prep: 10 minutes **Cooking:** 15 to 20 minutes **Makes:** several flat rounds
Pairs well with: cream cheese, smoked salmon, fresh butter

Cornmeal for dusting

2 cups prepared mashed potato made from russet or other jumbo potatoes

3 tablespoons melted unsalted butter

Pinch of salt

½ teaspoon Imperial Seasoning (page 27)

1 egg

1 to 2 cups all-purpose flour

1. Preheat the oven to 425°F and lightly sprinkle a baking sheet with cornmeal.

2. Mix all the remaining ingredients together in a large bowl, adding the flour a little at a time until you have a nice dough that isn't too sticky. With lightly floured hands, shape the dough into several flat rounds roughly 6 inches across, pressing flat on the baking sheet. Prick the breads a few times with a fork, and bake for 15 to 20 minutes, or until the top starts to turn golden brown.

3. The bread is best enjoyed the same day, but will keep for a little while if you are planning a foray into the wilds.

> **TIP**
>
> Try mixing up the flavor of this bread by adding in some different flours. Rye is the traditional Nord flour, but other hearty milled flours are also a safe bet. This recipe can also be made with either leftover mashed or baked potatoes—boiled potatoes are often too watery.

NUT AND SEED LOAF

Packed with protein and nutrition, a little slice of this loaf goes a long way. It's an ideal addition to the rations of any adventurers keen to make a name for themselves in the wilds of Tamriel, where an assortment of foraged ingredients can be added, such as ironwood nuts and seeds from an assortment of wildflowers.

LEVEL

Prep: 10 minutes **Cooking:** 45 minutes
Makes: 1 loaf **Pairs well with:** cream cheese, cured salmon, jams

2 cups mixed nuts (almonds, pistachios, pecans, pine nuts, hazelnuts, walnuts, etc.)

3 cups mixed seeds (poppy, chia, sesame, sunflower, millet, pumpkin, flax, etc.)

2 cups rolled oats

½ cup raisins or dried currants

4 eggs

1½ teaspoons sea salt

1 tablespoon apple cider vinegar

1. Preheat oven to 350°F, and line an 8.5-inch by 4.5-inch (1 pound) loaf pan with parchment paper, which will help lift the loaf out after cooking.

2. Combine all the ingredients in a large bowl, stirring to mix evenly. Gently pour the mixture into the prepared pan, pressing down with the back of a spoon to make sure it is tightly packed. Bake for about 45 minutes, or until the top is beginning to turn golden and the loaf sounds hollow when tapped. Remove from the oven and allow the bread to finish cooling in the pan before removing it from the pan to slice.

3. Because the loaf is so dense, thinner slices are advisable. Can be served as is or lightly toasted.

TIP

This recipe is easily adapted to whatever ingredients you have on hand—feel free to experiment!

RYE CRISPS

Many Nords make their living as fishermen, exporting their catch to taverns and large estates all over Skyrim. But fishing is long, hard work, so they need nourishing foodstuffs that last. These crisps are thin and flavorful, perfect with a little cream cheese and smoked fish.

LEVEL

Prep: 10 minutes **Rising:** 45 minutes **Cooking:** 30 minutes
Makes: 12 crisps **Pairs well with:** cream cheese, smoked fish, jams

1½ cup rye flour, plus more for rolling

1 teaspoon instant dry yeast

¼ cup rolled oats

¼ cup sesame seeds

1 tablespoon poppy seeds

1 teaspoon fennel seeds

1 teaspoon caraway seeds

Pinch of salt

½ cup water

1. In a large bowl, combine all of the ingredients except the water. Then gradually add in just a little water at a time, until the dough has a good consistency that isn't sticky or too dry. Turn out the dough onto a lightly floured surface and knead for several minutes, until it bounces back when poked. Cover with a towel and set aside in a warm place to rise for about 45 minutes, until roughly doubled in size.

2. Once the dough has risen, preheat oven to 400°F and set out a flat baking sheet. Divide the dough into 12 more or less equal balls. Toss each ball of dough with additional flour and press them into flat disks on your work surface. Roll each disk out very thin, about ¼ inch thick, flipping and turning occasionally to be sure the dough doesn't stick to your work surface.

3. Move the rolled-out disks to the baking sheet. Bake 4 at a time for about 10 minutes, or until the crisps are beginning to brown on the edges.

> **TIP**
>
> The seeds included here are just suggestions for a good place to start. Feel free to improvise or alter the recipe based on what you've got in the pantry.

LAVENDER AND HONEY BREAD

This is a popular bread in Whiterun, where lavender grows wild and countless beehives are kept to provide the Honningbrew Meadery with enough honey for their mead production. The honey and lavender are such a natural pairing that they are combined not only for the mead but also in this flavorful loaf.

LEVEL ⬡▭▭▭▭⬡

Prep: 15 minutes **Rising:** 1 hour **Baking:** 25 minutes **Makes:** 1 loaf
Pairs well with: Honningbrew Mead (page 162), fresh berry jam and butter

1¼ cups warm whole milk

¼ cup (½ stick) unsalted butter

⅓ cup honey

1 heaping tablespoon culinary lavender

2 teaspoons instant dry yeast

1 teaspoon salt

2 cups whole wheat flour

2 cups all-purpose flour

1. Lightly butter the sides of an 8.5-inch by 4.5-inch (1 pound) loaf pan and set aside. In a large bowl, combine the milk, butter, and honey, stirring until the honey has dissolved. Stir in the lavender, yeast, and salt, along with 1 cup of the flour. Continue adding flour 1 cup at a time until the dough is no longer sticky.

2. Turn the dough out onto a lightly floured surface and knead for several minutes, until the dough bounces back slightly when poked. Form into an oblong shape and settle gently into the loaf pan. Cover lightly with plastic and set somewhere warm to rise for about 1 hour, until roughly doubled in size and a nice shape.

3. Once the dough has risen, preheat the oven to 400°F and bake for 25 to 30 minutes, or until a toothpick inserted into the middle of the loaf comes out clean. Allow to cool before slicing.

> **TIP**
>
> Culinary lavender can be acquired from alchemists but is more readily purchased at health food stores or online.

Sea o[f]

Solitude

Dawnstar

Winterho..

Morthal

The Reach

Skyrim

Windhelm

Whiterun

Falkreath

N

SOUPS & STEWS

Riften

APPLE CABBAGE STEW

The Imperials prefer a version of this dish that uses red cabbage, which they say is sweeter, but true Nords are unwavering in their affection for this traditional recipe. It produces a richly flavored broth that is both nutritious and delicious, despite the limited ingredient list.

LEVEL

Cooking: 30 minutes **Makes:** about 4 servings
Pairs well with: cured sausages, cold beer

2 tablespoons unsalted butter

1 leek, white parts only, sliced thin

½ head green cabbage, chopped thin

1 teaspoon dried thyme, plus more for garnishing

6 cups chicken broth

1 or 2 apples, red or green, cored and diced

1. Melt the butter in a large sauté pan and add the leeks. Cook for a few minutes, until soft and just shy of browning, then add the cabbage.

2. Cook for about 10 minutes or until the cabbage has softened considerably. Add the thyme and broth, followed by the apple. Cook for about 15 minutes more, until the apples are softened to your taste. Garnish with an extra sprinkle of thyme to serve.

COASTAL CLAM CHOWDER

Nordic barnacles, clams, oysters, mudcrabs, and a variety of fish are often included in this chowder, depending on the catch of the day. Unsurprisingly, it's a popular staple in coastal cities such as Solitude and Winterhold, where every inn and tavern has a steaming cauldron of chowder going in the kitchen.

LEVEL

Prep: 5 minutes   **Cooking:** 1 hour
Makes: 4 servings   **Pairs well with:** Meadow Rye Bread (page 73)

¼ pound bacon, diced

2 medium russet or 2 large yellow potatoes, peeled and diced

1 leek, white and light green parts sliced

One 10-ounce can of baby clams or canned seafood mix, with their juices

1 teaspoon Imperial Seasoning (page 27)

2 cups fish broth

2 to 4 cups water, as needed

2 tablespoons unsalted butter

2 tablespoons all-purpose flour

1 cup whole milk

1. Cover the bottom of a large saucepan with the bacon, followed by layers of the potatoes, leeks, and clams or seafood mix with their juice. Sprinkle the Imperial Seasoning over the top, then pour in the fish broth. Add enough water until all of the ingredients are covered, and set over medium heat to cook for about 30 minutes, until potatoes are soft and flavors have melded together.

2. In a small saucepan over medium heat, melt the butter and stir in the flour. While whisking, add the milk and stir until it thickens. Pour this into the large pan with all the other ingredients and cook 5 to 10 more minutes to thicken the broth.

⬡ **TIP**

For a slightly more sophisticated version, cook some additional bacon to be extra crispy, crumble it, and add it as a garnish just before serving.

BRAISED RIB STEW WITH FARRO

This is one of Skyrim's most rustic soups, made in the far-flung small villages and hunting camps that lie a long way from cities, where only the most adventurous might wander and every bit of food is considered precious, with nothing wasted. The rib bones knocking about at the bottom of the pot might seem a little dubious, but they give the broth extra nutrients that are essential for surviving long spells of frigid temperatures. This dish is especially helpful during recovery if one has taken a farro in the knee.

LEVEL

Prep: 15 minutes   **Cooking:** at least 2 hours
Makes: 6 servings   **Pairs well with:** Garlic Bread (page 77)

2 pounds beef short ribs

1 tablespoon olive oil

¼ cup port wine

5 cups beef stock

1 or 2 medium carrots, peeled and diced

1 or 2 medium parsnips, peeled and diced

1 leek, white and light green parts sliced

2 cloves garlic, minced

½ cup farro or barley

Salt and pepper

1. Season the ribs liberally with salt and pepper. Add the oil to a medium saucepan over medium heat, then brown the ribs in the bottom of the pot. Pour in the port wine, followed by the stock. Bring to a boil and cook with the pot partially covered, for about 1 hour, occasionally skimming off excess fat from the top.

2. Add the carrots, parsnips, leeks, garlic, and the farro or barley, then cook for 1 hour more, or until the grains are tender and the meat has begun falling from the bone. At this point, if you like, you can pull the meat out, cut it into smaller chunks, and then add it back into the stew.

3. This soup, like many, is best the next day when flavors have been allowed to mingle. Place the soup in the refrigerator overnight. Then before reheating the next day, skim any remaining fat from the top of the pot.

POTATO CHEDDAR SOUP

This dish is a staple at every farmstead and crofter's cottage across Skyrim. Simple but hearty, it gives a bone-deep warmth that better prepares anyone for the day's labors ahead, be they adventuring, tending a shop, or working the fields.

LEVEL

Prep: 10 minutes **Cooking:** 30 minutes
Makes: 4 servings **Pairs well with:** Garlic Bread (page 77)

2 tablespoons unsalted butter

1 small onion, minced

2 tablespoons all-purpose flour

2 cups chicken broth, plus more as needed

½ cup whole milk

3 or 4 medium russet potatoes, peeled and cubed (about 1 pound)

½ cup shredded cheddar cheese

1 teaspoon Stormcloak Seasoning (page 25)

½ cup heavy cream

Cooked, crumbled bacon for garnishing (optional)

1. Melt the butter in a medium saucepan over medium heat. Add the onion and cook for several minutes, until the onion is soft and fragrant. Sprinkle the flour in and stir to combine before continuing to cook for a few minutes more, until the flour is fully incorporated.

2. Add the chicken broth and milk, followed by the cubed potatoes. Turn up the heat so the mixture simmers, and cook until the potatoes are quite soft, about 15 minutes. Using an immersion blender or a potato masher, blend the soup until it is an even texture. Add the cheddar cheese, Stormcloak Seasoning, and just enough of the cream to get the consistency you like. Ladle into serving dishes and top with crumbled bacon, if desired.

> **TIP**
>
> This recipe can easily be scaled up by simply adding roughly one additional potato for each serving, and increasing the liquid and cheese accordingly.

PEA SOUP

Nothing wards off the winter's chill like a nice, hearty soup. This is a popular option in the depths of winter, when fresh greens are harder to come by, but it still incorporates some of Skyrim's most popular ingredients as it uses dried peas and cured bacon, along with carefully stored leeks and carrots. The result is a simple but filling staple that sticks to the ribs.

LEVEL

Soaking: overnight **Prep:** 5 minutes **Cooking:** 2½ hours
Makes: 4 large servings **Pairs well with:** Cheese Scones (page 75), extra bacon

2 cups dried split peas

10 cups beef or vegetable broth

1 tablespoon olive oil

1 medium carrot, peeled and diced

1 leek, white and light green parts sliced

6 to 8 bacon strips

2 teaspoons dried marjoram

Salt and pepper

1. Soak the split peas in 6 cups of water overnight.

2. When you're ready to make the soup, drain the water from the peas and add them to a large soup pot along with the broth. Set over medium heat and allow to simmer for about 90 minutes, until peas have begun to soften.

3. While the peas are cooking, warm the olive oil in a medium sauté pan or skillet, and sauté the carrots and leeks for several minutes until they've started to soften. Remove from the heat and set aside.

4. Also while the peas simmer, in a large sauté pan or skillet, cook the bacon—the crunchier the better.

5. After the peas have cooked, add the carrots, leeks, and most of the bacon to the pot, reserving some bacon as a topping. Season to taste with salt and pepper, and add the marjoram. Cook for 1 hour more, stirring once in a while, and adding more broth if needed. The soup is ready when the peas have fallen apart and are completely soft.

VEGETABLE SOUP

Some might claim that an ordinary vegetable soup has no business being so powerfully healthy, but there's no arguing with results. While it might not cure everything that ails you (try a shrine for that), it comes pretty close. Every spoonful is loaded with native vegetables and packed with flavor.

LEVEL

Prep: 15 minutes   **Cooking:** 45 minutes
Makes: 6 to 8 servings   **Pairs well with:** Garlic Bread (page 77)

2 tablespoons unsalted butter

2 cloves garlic, minced

2 leeks, white and light green parts, sliced

3 large carrots, diced

2 cups peeled, chopped butternut squash, in small pieces

½ teaspoon salt

½ teaspoon Stormcloak Seasoning (page 25)

One (28-ounce) can diced tomatoes

½ cup pearl barley

4 cups vegetable broth

2 cups water

1 cup chopped carrot greens, kale, or other greens, in small pieces

1. Melt the butter in a large saucepan over medium heat, then add the garlic and leeks and cook until they are soft and fragrant, 5 to 10 minutes. Add the carrots and squash, stirring to coat with butter, followed by the salt and Stormcloak Seasoning. Add the tomatoes and barley, then pour in the vegetable broth and water.

2. Let the soup simmer for about 45 minutes, then check to see if the barley is cooked through. If not, cook a little longer. Just before serving, add the chopped greens and stir to incorporate.

TIP

For a more Imperial touch, add ½ teaspoon each ground cumin and curry powder.

POTAGE LE MAGNIFIQUE

**This Breton dish is one of many made famous in the recipe collection
Uncommon Taste, written by the ever-mysterious Gourmet. Its popularity is
no mystery, however, as its rich texture and deceptive simplicity showcase
a hearty soup that pairs perfectly with toasted bread and cheese. The only
danger is that it may make you weep with joy . . .**

LEVEL

Prep: 10 minutes   **Cooking:** 20 minutes
Makes: at least 4 servings   **Pairs well with:** toasted bread, sharp cheese

¼ cup (½ stick) unsalted
   butter

½ cup diced onion

1 or 2 cloves garlic, minced

1 cup diced and peeled
   medium carrots

½ cup all-purpose flour

2 cups chicken broth

2 cups beef broth

Salt and pepper

1. Melt the butter in a large saucepan over medium heat, then add the
   onion and garlic. Cook until soft and fragrant, about 3 to 5 minutes,
   then add the diced carrots, stirring to coat with butter.

2. Sprinkle the flour into the pan and stir to be sure there are no clumps
   remaining. Add the chicken and beef broth, and cook until the carrots
   are soft, about 15 minutes. Puree with an immersion blender (or in
   batches in a regular blender) until it has a nice, thick consistency,
   adding with extra broth if needed to get your preferred consistency.
   Season with salt and pepper to taste.

TIP

As the Gourmet suggests, it takes the imagination of a truly inspired chef to make this
dish sing, and the real magic to it is adding ingredients to your own taste. Play with
combinations of vegetables and spices until you find just the right combination for you.

Bruma

Cheyd

Colovian highlands

Chorrol

Cyrodiil

Imperial City

Skingrad

Kvatch

Bravil

N

Leyawi

MAIN COURSES

SEARED NORDIC BARNACLES

Most Nords, from Solitude to Windhelm, have at some point or another gone out to scour the coast for barnacles and oysters. Those hard shells hide delicious treasures, if you know how to prepare them, and their relative rarity makes them a highly sought-after ingredient.

LEVEL ◇▭▭▭▭◇

Marinating: 20 minutes **Cooking:** 20 minutes
Makes: 2 to 4 servings **Pairs well with:** chilled white wine

2 teaspoons crushed juniper berries

1 cup white wine

Splash of apple cider vinegar or white wine vinegar

1 pound sea scallops

2 or 3 bacon strips

6 tablespoons unsalted butter

2 cloves garlic, minced

2 tablespoons maple syrup

1. In a large bowl, combine the juniper berries, white wine, and vinegar to create a marinade. Add the scallops, turning to coat. Let sit for about 20 minutes while you prepare the bacon.

2. In a medium sauté pan or skillet over medium heat, cook the bacon until crispy. Transfer the bacon to paper towels to drain, then crumble into a small bowl and set aside. Drain the fat from the pan.

3. When you're ready to cook the scallops, melt the butter in the pan over medium heat. Remove the scallops from the marinade, reserving the liquid. Arrange some of the scallops in the pan, flat-side down, leaving some space in between them. Sear until they are a nice golden brown, roughly 3 minutes. Flip the scallops and cook for another 3 minutes to brown the other side. Remove to a separate plate and cook the rest of the scallops until all of the scallops have been cooked. Set aside while you finish up the sauce.

4. Add the garlic to the pan and cook until fragrant and golden brown, about 3 minutes. Add the reserved marinade liquid along with the maple syrup and simmer until the sauce is somewhat reduced and thickened, about 3 to 5 minutes.

5. To serve, sprinkle the crumbled bacon on a plate and set the scallops on top. Drizzle the sauce over the scallops.

BAKED WHITE RIVER SALMON

Salmon can be seen leaping up the current of the White River in great numbers, making them a popular ingredient for cooking. There are myriad ways to catch them—arrows and bolts work well, but a skillfully deployed destruction spell can yield a number of fish quickly. Simply baking the fish with some herbs will result in a delicious meal, but nobles often prefer it baked into a pastry case.

LEVEL ⬦▭▭▭▭▭

Prep: 15 minutes   **Cooking:** 25 to 30 minutes   **Makes:** 4 to 6 servings
Pairs well with: Garlic Bread (page 77), rice

3 tablespoons butter

1 leek, diced

1 to 2 medium carrots, diced

¼ cup heavy cream

½ teaspoon Stormcloak Seasoning (page 25), plus a little extra pepper to taste

2 to 3 tablespoons grated Parmesan cheese

1 sheet puff pastry, thawed

1 pound salmon fillet

1 egg, beaten

1. Begin by melting the butter in a medium saucepan over medium heat. Add the diced leek and carrots to the pan and cook for around 15 minutes, until the leeks are soft and the carrots are beginning to soften. Pour in the heavy cream then sprinkle in the ½ teaspoon of Stormcloak Seasoning and pepper. Let the mixture simmer for a minute or two until the cream has cooked down a bit and has been partially absorbed. Remove from heat and stir in the cheese. Set aside to cool.

2. Preheat the oven to 375°F and line a baking sheet with parchment paper.

3. Lay the puff pastry dough on a lightly floured surface. Roll out the dough a bit until you have a rectangle that is large enough to wrap around the whole salmon fillet. Sprinkle the remaining Stormcloak Seasoning over the middle of the dough, then place the salmon on top of the seasoning. Spread the vegetable mix evenly over the fish, then brush the edges of the dough with the beaten egg. Fold the long sides of the pastry over the fish and vegetables, overlapping the pastry in the middle, then press the egg-washed seam together. Brush the sides of the pastry with egg and tuck them over the top seam toward the middle as far as they will go, also pressing them down.

4. Gently flip the salmon onto the prepared baking sheet so that the seam is facing down. Lightly score the top of the dough only partway through with a sharp knife, then brush with the remaining egg. Bake for about 25 to 30 minutes, until the top is a nice golden brown. Let cool for a few minutes before slicing and serving.

CHICKEN DUMPLINGS

These dumplings are a specialty of many an inn across Skyrim, where travelers can enjoy them hot after a long day's journey, but they're also a popular pick in one's own homestead kitchen. In either case, the creamy filling has restorative properties, especially washed down with a flagon of the local specialty.

LEVEL ◇▭▭▭▭▭▭◇

Prep: 1 hour **Baking:** 30 minutes **Makes:** 4 dumplings
Pairs well with: Pea Soup (page 99), strong mead, fried potatoes

6 chicken drumsticks (about 2 cups cooked meat)

2 tablespoons butter

1 leek, both white and light green parts sliced into thin half-moons

1 or 2 cloves garlic, minced

1 medium carrot, peeled and diced

½ teaspoon Stormcloak Seasoning (page 25)

1 tablespoon all-purpose flour

¾ cup heavy cream

¼ cup shredded cheddar cheese

Salt and pepper

1 recipe Rye Pie Dough (page 39)

1 egg, beaten, for glazing

1. Preheat the oven to 375°F and place the drumsticks on a baking sheet. Bake for 30 minutes, then flip and return to the oven for another 30 minutes, until cooked through.

2. While the drumsticks cook, melt the butter in a large sauté pan or skillet over medium heat, then add the leeks. Cook for several minutes, until the leeks are soft but not browning. Add the garlic, carrot, and Stormcloak Seasoning, and cook for another couple of minutes, until the carrots have softened a bit. Sprinkle the mixture with flour, then stir to combine completely. Gradually pour in the heavy cream, stirring all the while, and when you have a nice thick consistency, remove from the heat and stir in the cheese. Season with salt and pepper to taste.

3. When the chicken is done cooking, strip the meat from the bones and tear into small pieces. Add these to the cream filling mixture, stirring to incorporate. Lower the oven to 350°F.

4. Roll out the Rye Pie Dough to ⅛ of an inch thick and shape into a rough square. Cut the dough into 4 even squares, adding a little dough here and there if needed to maintain the shape.

Continued on page 113 . . .

5. Working one at a time, lay a square of dough out on a clean baking sheet lined with parchment paper. Divide the filling into 4 equal portions, and scoop one portion onto the square of dough, spreading it out evenly but leaving at least ½ inch bare around the edges.

6. Dampen those bare edges with a little water, then take 2 of the corners and fold them toward the middle. Pinch together, then repeat with the other 2 corners. This should create seams that you can pinch closed. Repeat with the remaining dough and filling.

7. Brush the dumplings with the beaten egg and bake for about 30 minutes, or until the tops are just starting to turn golden. Allow to cool slightly before enjoying.

> **TIP**

You can skip the first step of this recipe if you already have leftover chicken. You'll need about 2 cups.

COMPANIONS MEATBALL BAKE

This deceptively simple dish is a favorite among Whiterun's Companions, where it is always served in a round shape to symbolize their equality with one another. They fight together, drink together, and, perhaps most importantly, feast together in the hall of Jorrvaskr. As the Companions are proficient hunters, these meatballs might be made of whatever has been freshly caught, be it bear, venison, boar, mammoth, or what have you.

LEVEL

Prep: 15 minutes   **Cooking:** 30 minutes
Makes: 4 servings   **Pairs well with:** rustic bread, good ale

1 pound baby potatoes

2 tablespoons vegetable oil

1 pound ground beef or other meat

½ cup breadcrumbs

1 egg

1 tablespoon sour cream

1 clove garlic, minced

¼ teaspoon Stormcloak Seasoning (page 25)

1 cup boiling water

¼ cup sour cream

2 to 3 tablespoons tomato paste

1. Preheat the oven to 450°F and rub the potatoes all over with the oil. Place them on a baking sheet and roast for about 15 minutes, until they are somewhat soft but not cooked all the way through.

2. While the potatoes are baking, make the meatballs by combining the ground meat, breadcrumbs, egg, sour cream, garlic, and Stormcloak Seasoning. Mix thoroughly and form into balls roughly the size of the potatoes. When the potatoes are done, remove them from the oven and turn the heat down to 350°F.

3. Cut the potatoes roughly into ½-inch-thick rounds, keeping the slices all together in a potato shape. Alternate the potatoes and meatballs in a casserole dish until the dish is full. Mix together the boiling water, sour cream, and tomato paste in a small bowl or measuring cup, then pour over the meatballs and potatoes until the liquid comes most of the way up the sides of the casserole. Bake for 25 to 30 minutes, until the meatballs are cooked through.

> **TIP**
>
> These proportions make enough for four stalwart warriors, but the recipe can easily be scaled up for a larger gathering.

ELSWEYR FONDUE

Although the Khajiit are known for their sweet tooth, this is one of their more savory recipes. Rich and creamy, this pot of melted cheese is a treat no Khajiit can resist, even without the inclusion of illegal moonsugar.

LEVEL

Prep: 10 minutes **Makes:** enough for 4
Pairs well with: crusty rustic bread, apples

2 cloves garlic, halved

1 cup semisweet white wine

2 teaspoons cornstarch

1 pound Gruyère cheese, grated

Pinch of ground nutmeg

Snacks for dipping

1. Rub the sides of a small saucepan with the garlic, then add the garlic halves to the pan. In a small bowl, whisk together the wine and cornstarch, then add to the pan and bring up to just under boiling over medium heat.

2. Remove from the heat and gradually add the cheese, stirring as you go until it is all melted and combined. Top with a pinch of ground nutmeg. Serve hot with a variety of delicious things to dip in the fondue such as crusty bread, apples, dried fruits, pretzels, and other sweet and savory snacks. Rewarm gently if needed during your meal.

FESTIVAL HAND PIES

These savory little hand pies are easily transported and easily eaten on the go, making them a common snack at festivals and other social gatherings throughout Skyrim. They are especially popular at the Fire Festival at the bard's college in Solitude. With a flaky crust and rich filling, it's a challenge to eat just one. Wash it down with a little of San's Spiced Wine, another local favorite.

LEVEL

Prep: 20 minutes   **Baking:** 25 minutes
Makes: about 12   **Pairs well with:** San's Spiced Wine (page 171)

1 tablespoon unsalted butter

1 or 2 cloves garlic, minced

½ teaspoon Stormcloak Seasoning (page 25)

¾ pound ground beef

½ cup sour cream

1 cup cooked white rice

½ cup shredded cheddar cheese

Salt and pepper to taste

1 recipe Rye Pie Dough (page 39)

Heavy cream for brushing

1. Melt the butter in a medium sauté pan or skillet over medium heat. Add the garlic and cook until golden and fragrant, several minutes, then add the Stormcloak Seasoning and ground beef. Cook until all the meat is browned, then lower the heat and stir in the sour cream and rice. When those are both incorporated, remove from heat and stir in the cheddar cheese, and a dash of salt and pepper to taste. Allow the mixture to cool for about 10 minutes or so.

2. Preheat the oven to 350°F and line a large baking sheet with parchment paper. On a lightly floured surface, roll out the Rye Pie Dough to no more than ⅛ inch thick. Using a round 5-inch cutter, cut out an even number of circles and move half of them to the prepared baking sheet. Repeat until most of the dough is used.

3. Pile a small heap of the filling in the center of each dough round, leaving a little room around the edge. Place another dough round on top, pressing the seams together, then crimp the edge with the tines of a fork. Decorate the pies with any extra dough, if you like, then brush with heavy cream. Bake for around 25 minutes, or until the tops are starting to turn golden. Allow to cool for several minutes before eating.

GOATHERD'S PIE

Although cows are the predominant herd animal kept in Skyrim, goats are better suited to finding forage on the rockier slopes and colder parts of the region. Their sure-footedness gives them the ability to escape sabre cats and cave bears, while their docile nature makes them ideal for the farmstead. That, and their cheese and meat are delicious.

LEVEL

Prep: 35 minutes   **Cooking:** 30 minutes
Makes: 1 pie, 4 to 6 servings   **Pairs well with:** dark beer

Filling:

2 cups mixed vegetables, such as peas, carrots, etc.

1 tablespoon olive oil

1 leek, white parts only, sliced

2 cloves garlic, minced

1½ pounds ground lamb, goat, or beef

2 tablespoons tomato paste

2 tablespoons all-purpose flour

½ cup beef broth

Salt and pepper

Topping:

2 large russet potatoes, peeled and diced

3 tablespoons unsalted butter

½ cup heavy cream

1 egg

Salt and pepper

TIP

The trick to a great shepherd's pie is to prepare all the various parts of it separately, then bring them together just before the pie goes into the oven; this involves keeping track of 3 separate pots, but is worth the effort.

1. To make the filling: Preheat the oven to 400°F and bring a small pot of water to a boil.

2. Drop in the mixed vegetables and let them cook for several minutes just to start softening them up. Root vegetables will need a little longer than fresh peas. When the vegetables have softened some, strain them and run under cold water to stop the cooking. Transfer the vegetables to the bottom of a casserole dish and set aside.

3. To make the topping: In a large pot of boiling water, cook the potatoes until they are soft, 10 to 15 minutes depending on their size. Strain and mash, adding the remaining ingredients for the topping, and season to taste with salt and pepper.

Continued on page 123 . . .

4. While the vegetables and potatoes are boiling, heat the olive oil in a large sauté pan or skillet over medium heat. Add the leeks and garlic, then cook for several minutes, until soft and fragrant and only just beginning to brown. Add these to the vegetables in the casserole dish, stirring to make sure everything is evenly mixed.

5. In the same pan you used for the leeks and garlic, add the ground meat and begin to brown over medium-high heat, stirring to make sure all the meat cooks evenly. Once the meat is browned, stir in the tomato paste. Sprinkle the flour over the top and stir that in as well, until it has a thick consistency. Add the broth and cook for a few more minutes. Season with salt and pepper to taste.

6. Layer the cooked meat over top of the vegetables in the casserole dish. Top with the mashed potatoes, spreading them out in a decorative pattern. Bake to for 30 minutes, or until the potato top is starting to brown.

KWAMA EGG QUICHE

Originally only known in Vvardenfell, this recipe traveled with Dunmer fleeing Morrowind after the Red Mountain's eruption and has been well received throughout much of Tamriel, albeit with various regional tweaks to the ingredient list. The lightly seasoned filling and crisp crust can satisfy even the pickiest palate.

LEVEL

Prep: 15 minutes   **Cooking:** 1 hour   **Makes:** 1 quiche, about 8 servings
Pairs well with: a fried breakfast, strong tea or coffee

1 recipe Rye Pie Dough
  (page 39)

1 tablespoon salted butter

1 or 2 cloves garlic, minced

2 medium tomatoes, divided

1 medium kwama egg or
  4 chicken eggs

½ cup whole milk

1 cup shredded cheddar
  cheese

½ cup grated Parmesan
  cheese

½ teaspoon salt

1. Preheat the oven to 350°F. Roll out the Rye Pie Dough to about ⅛ inch thick, and gently drape over a tart or pie pan. Press carefully into the bottom and sides of the pan, and trim off any excess. Prick the bottom of the pastry several times with a fork to prevent it from bubbling up.

2. Melt the butter in a medium sauté pan or skillet over medium heat. Add the garlic and cook for several minutes, until slightly browned. Chop one of the tomatoes, add to the pan, and cook for another few minutes, until the tomatoes are soft, but not yet falling apart. Remove from heat and set aside.

3. In a large bowl, whisk together the eggs, milk, cheddar cheese, Parmesan cheese, and salt. Pour this mixture into the pastry shell, slice the remaining tomato, then evenly layer the tomatoes on top of the filling. Bake for about an hour, or until the egg top is golden and puffy around the tomatoes. Allow to cool for 10 minutes before slicing and serving.

ORSIMER VENISON

Because of their tight-knit tribal communities, the Orsimer cook many communal meals where a large central dish is shared among many individuals. This recipe is a prime example of such a meal, especially as venison is one of their staple ingredients, being plentiful around their scattered strongholds.

LEVEL ▨▨▨▨

Prep: 5 minutes **Cooking:** 10 minutes **Makes:** 2 large portions
Pairs well with: rice pilaf, Hot Spiced Cider (page 169)

2 tablespoons olive oil, divided

1 pound venison, cut into bite-size pieces

2 tablespoons cornstarch or all-purpose flour

1 teaspoon salt, plus more for seasoning

1 teaspoon pepper, plus more for seasoning

1 or 2 cloves garlic

2 teaspoons grated fresh ginger

¼ cup soy sauce

¼ cup packed brown sugar

Splash of water

Pinch of ground cumin

Pinch of red pepper flakes

1. Pour 1 tablespoon of the oil into a large sauté pan or skillet over medium heat. In a medium bowl, toss the venison pieces with the cornstarch, salt, and pepper. When the oil is hot, add the venison to the pan and cook until done, turning the meat over occasionally, for about 5 minutes. Remove the meat and set aside.

2. Pour the remaining 1 tablespoon oil into the pan and add the garlic and ginger. Cook for a minute or so, until starting to brown, then add the soy sauce, brown sugar, water, cumin, and red pepper flakes. Cook the sauce for a few minutes until it begins to thicken a little, then add the venison back into the pan. Cook for 1 more minute or so, stirring occasionally so that all the meat is covered equally with sauce. Add more salt and pepper to taste if necessary before serving over a bed of rice pilaf.

JUNIPER LAMB CHOPS

Juniper grows best in the southwest of Skyrim, but its sharp flavor is enjoyed across the entire region. Sheep are commonly found in herds in Tamriel, so procuring lamb chops shouldn't be difficult. Just be sure to always carry a few apples with you in order to lure them in your direction.

LEVEL

Marinating: at least 2 hours **Cooking:** 15 minutes
Makes: 2 to 4 servings **Pairs well with:** Double-Baked Potatoes (page 53)

- 4 lamb chops, ¾ of an inch thick
- 2 teaspoons salt, plus more to taste
- 1 clove garlic, minced
- 1 tablespoon juniper berries, crushed and measured
- 1 cup dark beer, such as a stout or porter
- 2 cups beef broth
- 1 bay leaf
- Pinch of ground cloves
- ¼ cup honey
- 1 tablespoon unsalted butter
- Pepper

1. Combine all the ingredients except for the butter in a plastic zip-top bag or glass container with a lid and set in the refrigerator to marinate for at least 2 hours.

2. When you are ready to cook, take the lamb from the marinade and reserve the liquid. Melt the butter in a medium sauté pan or skillet over medium heat. Season the lamb chops with salt and pepper, then cook them for about 5 to 10 minutes, turning occasionally, until cooked through to your desired doneness. Remove to a plate and keep warm.

3. Make the sauce by straining the marinating liquid into the pan and reducing over medium heat for about 10 minutes, or until noticeably thickened. Plate the lamb chops and pour the sauce over the top.

HORKER LOAF

While horker meat might not be everyone's first pick, it sustains many a coastal family. It's considered lucky to eat the roasted garlic "tusks" at the top of the loaf, and children will often compete with one another to get them.

LEVEL ◇▨▨▨▨◇

Prep: 10 minutes **Cooking:** 40 minutes **Makes:** 1 loaf, 4 to 6 servings
Pairs well with: Double-Baked Potatoes (page 53), Baby Carrots in Moonsugar Glaze (page 43), Imperial Mushroom Sauce (page 37)

One 3.75-ounce tin smoked oysters

5 cloves garlic, divided

1 large carrot, peeled and chopped

1½ pounds ground beef

½ cup breadcrumbs

⅓ cup heavy cream

1 egg

1 teaspoon Stormcloak Seasoning (page 25)

1 teaspoon salt

1 teaspoon pepper

5 bacon slices

1. Preheat the oven to 425°F degrees and line a baking sheet with parchment paper.

2. Mince 2 cloves of the garlic, then pulse the oysters, minced garlic, and carrot several times in a food processor until there are no large chunks. In a large bowl, combine the pureed mixture with the ground beef, breadcrumbs, heavy cream, egg, Stormcloak Seasoning, salt, and pepper. Mix thoroughly, then form into a slightly oblong dome, no higher than 4 inches, on the prepared baking sheet.

3. Gently press the 3 remaining garlic cloves into the top of the loaf. Then, working from just next to the garlic, begin laying the bacon slices across the short side of the loaf, 2 on each side. Lay one final strip over the garlic to keep it from burning.

4. Bake for about 40 minutes. Peel back the top piece of bacon to reveal the garlic tusks before serving.

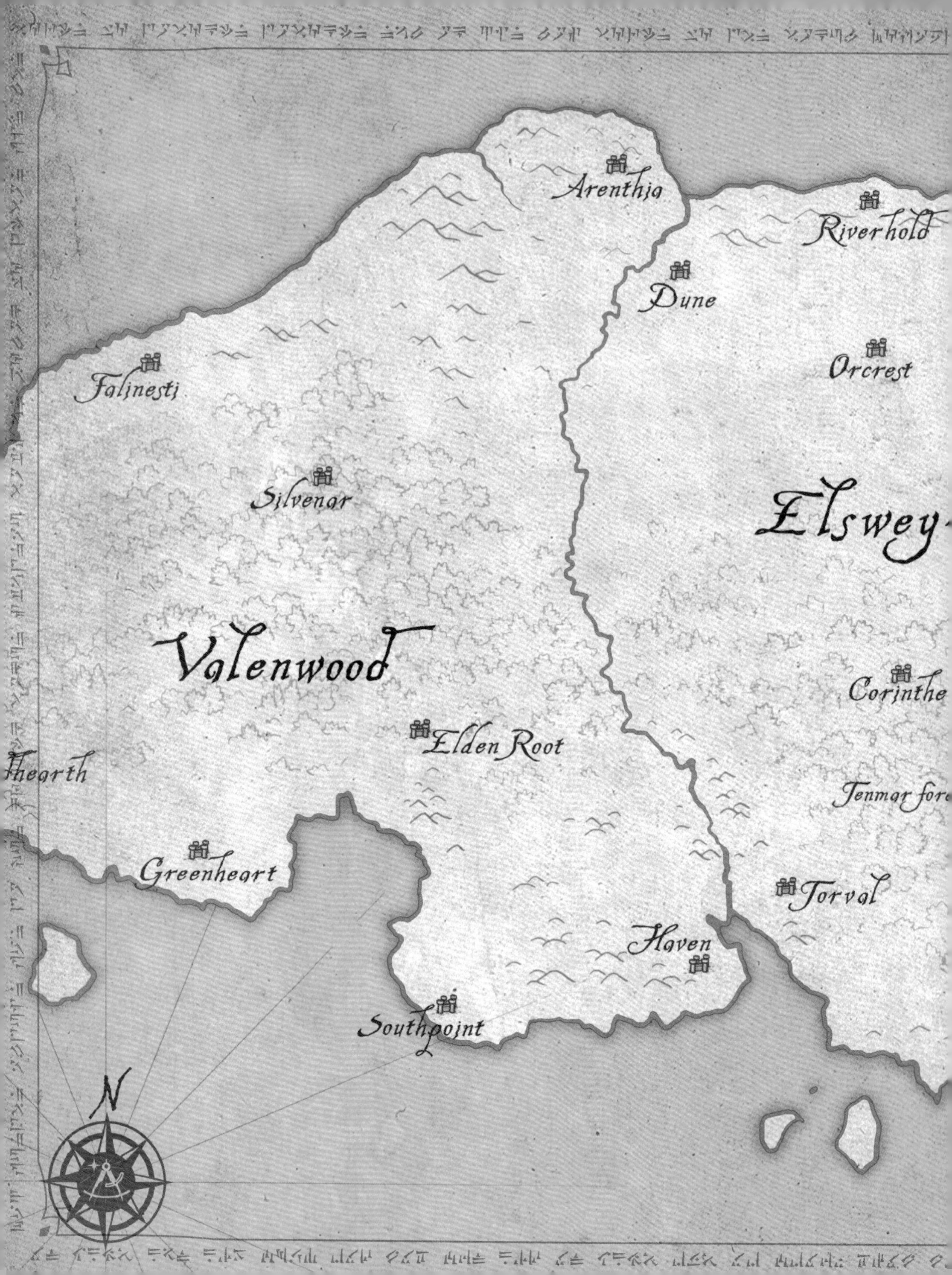

Arenthia

Riverhold

Dune

Orcrest

Falinesti

Silvenar

Elswey

Valenwood

Corinthe

Thearth

Elden Root

Jenmar fore

Greenheart

Torval

Haven

Southpoint

N

DESSERTS

Rimmen

Senchal

HONEY NUT TREAT

Honey nut treats are one of the most loved sweets in all of Skyrim. Made with a variety of delicious ingredients from different parts of Tamriel, they're actually quite easy and quick to make at your own hearth.

LEVEL

Prep: 15 minutes **Makes:** about 9 balls or 3 skewers
Pairs well with: a large breakfast before adventuring, picnics

1 cup pitted dates

½ cup golden raisins

1 cup sliced almonds

1 cup rolled oats

¼ cup honey

¼ cup smooth or crunchy peanut butter

Pinch of salt

Pinch of ground cinnamon

1. Pulse the dates and raisins in a food processor until there are no large pieces remaining. Add the almonds and oats and pulse a few more times to incorporate; you can also dice the dried fruits by hand if need be.

2. In a large bowl, heat the honey and peanut butter in a microwave or on top of a double boiler until they are a little runny. Add the fruit and nut mixture, plus the salt and cinnamon, to the bowl and mix vigorously until you have a thick consistency. Scoop out small pieces of the mix, squash in between your hands, then roll into balls. Set on a clean plate. Repeat until everything is used up, then thread onto skewers.

3. The rougher your skewer, the better the treats will stick, I learned, but I didn't *quite* have time to go out and whittle down a twig. If your treats start to slide, I suggest you just eat them a little quicker, or add a few more oats.

TIP

You can substitute in any nuts or nut butters you like in this recipe, and it'll be just as tasty.

BIRCH COOKIES

Birch trees are some of the hardy varieties that still thrive in the cold Skyrim climate. These cookies honor those stalwart trees and their enterprising spirit with miniature versions of the birch logs that burn in many a hearthfire, keeping residents warm and snug.

LEVEL

Prep: 30 minutes **Chilling:** 1 hour **Baking:** 12 minutes **Makes:** about 18 cookies
Pairs well with: Sweet Nog (page 179)

Dough:

¾ cup sugar

¾ cup (1½ sticks) unsalted butter

2 teaspoons vanilla extract

1 egg

Pinch of salt

1 teaspoon ground nutmeg

2½ cups all-purpose flour

Frosting:

3 tablespoons unsalted butter, softened

1½ cups powdered sugar

½ teaspoon vanilla extract

Dash of rum

4 to 6 teaspoons heavy cream

Ground nutmeg, for dusting

To make the dough:

1. In a medium bowl, cream together the sugar and butter, then stir in the vanilla, egg, salt, and nutmeg. Gradually add in the flour until you have a dough that is no longer sticky, but isn't yet crumbly and dry. Form into a flat disk, wrap in plastic, and refrigerate for about an hour.

2. When you are ready to bake, preheat the oven to 350°F and line a baking sheet with parchment paper. Working with one-half of the dough at a time, roll it out into a rope no more than an inch thick. Cut at slight angles into pieces about 3 to 4 inches long and set on the prepared baking sheet. Use any extra dough to add little branches to some of the logs. Don't worry if they look a little odd—the frosting will cover them nicely. Repeat with the remaining dough.

3. Bake the cookies for about 12 minutes, until they are firming up and just starting to turn golden on the edges. Move to a cooling rack.

To make the frosting:

4. While the cookies are baking, beat together the butter, powdered sugar, vanilla, rum, and just enough cream to make a nice, thick frosting. When the cookies are completely cool, spread a little of the frosting on each one, smoothing out with a spoon or fingertip. Drag the tines of a fork lightly along the frosting to give the impression of tree bark, then dust with a little extra nutmeg.

HONEYCOMB BRITTLE

Honeycomb fresh from the hive is a rare treat for children and adults alike, and gives its name to this delicious confection. Light and crispy, with toasted honey flavors, this is sure to be a popular conclusion to any meal.

LEVEL

Prep: 5 minutes **Cooking:** 15 minutes **Makes:** Servings vary
Pairs well with: ice cream, chocolate cakes, hot tea

1 tablespoon salted butter

1 tablespoon baking soda

1 cup sugar

1 cup honey

Splash of apple cider vinegar

1. Line a baking sheet with parchment paper and butter the paper, or line it with a silicone pad. Measure out the butter and baking soda and set within easy reach. If you have a candy thermometer, it's recommended that you use it for this recipe. Read through the rest of the instructions, as they involve hot sugar and careful timing.

2. Combine the sugar, honey, and apple cider vinegar in a large saucepan with tall sides. Begin heating the mixture over medium-high heat until it reaches 300°F. Remove from heat and quickly stir in the butter. Follow this with the baking soda but be careful as you add it, as the baking soda will cause the whole mixture to bubble and expand wildly. Stir thoroughly for about 15 seconds to be sure there are no lumps of soda remaining, then quickly but carefully pour out the mixture onto the prepared baking sheet.

3. Allow the brittle to cool completely on the sheet before breaking it up into pieces to serve.

LONG TAFFY TREAT

Until recently, the recipe for this confection was so closely guarded that it was impossible to make at home and could only be obtained by nefarious means. Thankfully, a careless Whiterun guard let slip the secret after one too many ales, so now it can be enjoyed much more widely.

LEVEL

Active time: 45 minutes **Makes:** Servings vary **Pairs well with:** fruity tea

⅔ cup boiling water

1 herbal tea bag

1 cup sugar

¾ cup honey

½ teaspoon salt

2 tablespoons unsalted butter, at room temperature, plus more for stretching

1. Line a baking sheet with a silicone pad or heavily coat a baking sheet with butter.

2. Steep the teabag in the boiling water for several minutes, until you have a nice strong brew. Remove the tea bag and pour the tea into a medium stock pot along with the sugar, honey, and salt. Over medium-high heat, bring the mixture up to 255°F, then remove from the heat and quickly stir in the butter. Pour onto the prepared baking sheet.

3. Using a buttered knife or spatula, move the taffy mixture around until it has cooled enough to handle. Begin stretching it between your hands, twisting the taffy a half turn each time you stretch it, doubling back on itself. This process takes several minutes, so hang in there.

4. As the taffy begins to set, it will turn opaque and become harder to handle. At this point, stretch it into thin ropes no more than ½ inch wide and cut into your desired lengths. Store in an airtight container, if there's any left uneaten.

TIP

Snowberry-flavored taffy is the most popular in Skyrim. You can use any tea you like to flavor the taffy, but any berry infusion is especially tasty and often imparts that classic pink color. Experiment to find your favorite flavor.

HONEY PUDDING

Originally a Khajiit dish, this pudding has evolved without the moonsugar, letting the natural sweet flavors of the honey shine through. Different varieties of honey will each give a slightly different flavor, depending on the flowers it was made from.

LEVEL ◇▭▭▭▭◇

Prep: 10 minutes   **Cooking:** 10 minutes   **Chilling:** 1 hour   **Makes:** 4 servings
Pairs well with: Canis Root Tea (page 181)

2 cups whole milk

1 whole vanilla bean or 1 teaspoon vanilla extract

½ cup honey

1 cup heavy cream or whipping cream

3 tablespoons cornstarch

3 egg yolks

Pinch of salt

1. Pour the milk into a medium pot over medium heat. If using a whole vanilla bean, split the bean down the middle with a sharp knife and scrape out the seeds. Add the seeds and the pod to the pot of milk, and bring to just under a boil. If using vanilla extract, simply add the extract to the milk. Add the honey and stir for a few minutes to allow the vanilla to steep into the milk.

2. In a medium bowl, whisk together the heavy cream or whipping cream, cornstarch, egg yolks, and salt. While whisking, pour a little of the hot milk into the bowl to temper the mixture, then pour everything back into the pot. Turn the heat up a little and cook for about 5 minutes more, stirring all the while, until the mixture has thickened noticeably. Remove from the heat, strain through a mesh sieve into a clean bowl, and cover with plastic. Refrigerate for at least 1 hour to help the pudding set.

OATMEAL RAISIN SHORTBREAD

Sometimes the simplest recipes can be the most rewarding. While variations can be found across Skyrim, this particular recipe comes from a little fishing cottage outside of Winterhold. Sweet and buttery, these little iced shortbreads are a perfect pick-me-up in the morning or in the afternoon with a cup of tea. These shortbreads can be cut into any shape you desire from simple circles, squares, and triangles to more adventurous concepts. If you're feeling creative, try your hand at creating shapes such as a snow bear, ice wraith, or even Alduin the World Eater.

LEVEL

Prep: 10 minutes   **Baking:** 15 minutes
Makes: about a dozen   **Pairs well with:** cold fresh milk, Canis Root Tea (page 181)

Cookies:

½ cup (1 stick) unsalted butter, softened

½ cup granulated sugar

½ teaspoon Nord Spices (page 23)

½ cup rolled oats

½ cup raisins

1 cup all-purpose flour

Icing:

¼ cup powdered sugar

1 tablespoon heavy cream

Maple syrup or honey as needed

To make the cookies:

1. In a large bowl, cream together the butter and sugar, then add the Nord Spices, oats, and raisins. Begin adding the flour, mixing until you have a consistency just shy of too crumbly. Roll out to a little over ¼ inch thick and cut into your desired shapes. Place these on a baking sheet lined with parchment paper. Refrigerate for about 30 minutes.

2. Preheat the oven to 350°F, and after the shortbread has chilled, bake for about 10 minutes, until the edges are just turning golden. Remove from the oven and allow to cool on a wire rack.

To make the icing:

3. While the shortbread is cooling, combine the powdered sugar and heavy cream in a small bowl. Add just a little bit of maple syrup or honey at a time until the icing coats the back of a spoon, but is still a little runny. Drizzle over the shortbreads once they are completely cool.

SHEOGORATH'S STRAWBERRY TARTS

Wine in a fruit tart? That's madness! Or genius. Or perhaps a bit
of both, because the line between the two is very narrow. The line
of neighbors waiting for your summery dessert, however, will
probably grow longer with time.

LEVEL

Prep: 20 minutes **Baking:** 20 minutes **Makes:** 1 tart, about 8 servings
Pairs well with: a picnic in an alternate reality, whipped cream

1 recipe Sweet Crostata
Dough (page 39)

1 quart strawberries

¼ cup granulated sugar

¼ cup port wine

A few sprigs of fresh thyme

8 ounces mascarpone

¼ cup powdered sugar

2 tablespoons heavy cream

1. Preheat the oven to 375°F. Roll out the Sweet Crostata Dough to
   about ¼ inch thick or a little less, then drape over an 8- or 9-inch
   tart tin. Press into the sides of the tin and trim off any excess dough.
   Prick the bottom of the tart several times with a fork and place a
   few pie weights or dried beans in the tart to keep the dough from
   bubbling up, then bake for 15 to 20 minutes, or until the crust has
   started to turn golden. Remove from the oven and let cool.

2. While the crust is baking, trim the tops off the strawberries and slice
   them thinly. Toss the strawberry slices with the granulated sugar
   in a small bowl and let sit for around 15 minutes, until they start
   to release their juice. Strain the extra strawberry juice into a small
   saucepan and set the strawberries aside.

3. Take the saucepan with the strawberry juice and add the port and
   thyme, then place over medium heat and cook until it has reduced
   by half to create a port glaze. Set aside to cool.

4. In a medium bowl, combine the mascarpone, powdered sugar, and
   heavy cream, beating until combined.

5. When the tart shell has cooled completely, spread the mascarpone
   mix evenly across the bottom. Layer the strawberries on top, then
   drizzle with the port glaze.

APPLE COBBLER

That the gnarled and twisted trees in Skyrim's orchards still produce such bounty of fruits is nothing short of a marvel. Their round green and red apples are sold and stored all across the region, making their way into various desserts and drinks or eaten raw as a quick, healthy snack.

LEVEL

Prep: 15 minutes **Cooking:** 40 minutes **Makes:** 6 to 8 servings
Pairs well with: vanilla ice cream, Custard Sauce (page 29)

Filling:

¾ cup packed brown sugar

2 tablespoons cornstarch

2 teaspoons Nord Spices
(page 23)

5 or 6 medium Honeycrisp
apples, peeled, cored, and
sliced into wedges

Topping:

1½ cups all-purpose flour

1 cup rolled oats

½ cup granulated sugar

1 tablespoon baking powder

1 teaspoon salt

5 tablespoons unsalted butter

1 cup buttermilk

To make the filling:

1. Preheat the oven to 375°F. Mix together the brown sugar, cornstarch, and Nord Spices in a small bowl. Place the sliced apples into a 9-inch by 13-inch baking dish, then sprinkle with the sugar mixture. Stir to make sure the apples are completely coated. Set aside while you make the topping.

To make the topping:

2. Combine the flour, oats, sugar, baking powder, and salt in a medium bowl, then rub or cut in the butter until the whole mixture looks crumbly. Gradually add the buttermilk until you have a nice thick batter with no dry spots. Using a large spoon, drop dollops of the batter on top of the apples.

3. Bake for 35 to 40 minutes, or until the tops are turning golden and the dough is cooked through. Allow to cool for about 10 minutes before serving.

SNOWBERRY CROSTATA

This rustic berry tart is most commonly made over the hearthfires of home kitchens, but can occasionally be found for sale in a few taverns and inns as well. The recipe makes a dessert that's just this side of tart, and perfect to share with your traveling companions.

LEVEL

Prep: 15 minutes   **Baking:** 40 minutes   **Makes:** 8 to 10 servings
Pairs well with: San's Spiced Wine (page 171), assorted cheeses and nuts

1 recipe Sweet Crostata Dough (page 39)

1 cup granulated sugar

2 eggs

1 teaspoon Nord Spices (page 23)

½ cup (1 stick) unsalted butter, melted

1 to 2 teaspoons almond extract

1 cup all-purpose flour

12 ounces fresh cranberries

½ cup sliced almonds

1 egg, beaten, for glazing

1 tablespoon powdered sugar for dusting

1. Preheat the oven to 325°F and line a large baking sheet with parchment paper. Roll out the Sweet Crostata Dough in a roughly round shape to about ⅛ inch thick, and drape it over a large baking sheet lined with parchment paper. Leave the excess dough draped over the sides and prick the bottom all over with a fork to keep it from bubbling up too much. Cover with plastic wrap and place in the refrigerator while you make the filling.

2. In a medium bowl, combine the granulated sugar, eggs, Nord Spices, melted butter, and almond extract. Whisk in the flour until you have a thick batter.

3. Take the dough from the refrigerator and pour half the cranberries onto it, spreading them evenly but leaving a little space around the edge of the dough. Pour the batter over the cranberries. Sprinkle the almonds over the filling, then top with the remaining cranberries, pressing them gently into the batter.

4. Fold the hanging edges of the dough inward and over the filling to keep the berries contained. Brush with the beaten egg to glaze. Bake for about 40 minutes, or until a toothpick poked into the middle of the crostata comes out clean. Allow to cool for about 10 minutes, then dust with powdered sugar.

BOILED CREME TREAT

Nearly as iconic as sweetrolls but not as often stolen, these boiled creme treats are quite popular in Skyrim and can be purchased from most vendors worth their salt. The fluffy sweet dough around a creamy custard filling makes for a substantial little dessert that's so delicious, you'll think you've died and gone to Sovngarde.

LEVEL

Prep: 15 minutes   **Rising:** 1½ hours   **Baking:** 15 minutes
Makes: 10 treats   **Pairs well with:** Sweet Nog (page 179), afternoon tea

¼ cup (½ stick) unsalted butter, melted

1¼ cups warm milk

½ cup sugar

2 teaspoons active dry yeast

¼ teaspoon salt

1 teaspoon ground cardamom

4 cups all-purpose flour

1 egg, beaten with a little milk, for glazing

1 recipe Custard Sauce (page 29)

1. Preheat the oven to 350°F, and combine the melted butter, milk, sugar, and yeast in a medium bowl and stir until the yeast is dissolved. Add the salt and cardamom, then gradually mix in the flour until you have a dough that isn't too sticky to handle. Turn out onto a lightly floured surface and knead for several minutes, until the dough bounces back when poked. Cover with plastic and set somewhere warm to rise for about 1 hour, or until doubled in size.

2. Once the dough has risen, punch it back down and divide into 10 equal pieces. Shape each of these into a slightly flattened ball and place on a baking sheet lined with parchment paper. Cover with plastic again and allow to rise for about 30 minutes more, until light and puffy.

3. Once the buns have risen, using a small glass or your thumb, press down and outward into the middle of each bun to form a hollow indent in the dough. Brush the buns all over with the beaten egg with milk, then pour a little of the custard filling into each indent. Bake for 12 to 15 minutes, until the buns are a nice golden brown.

SPICED ROOT CAKE

Sometimes the humblest vegetables can shine in unexpected ways, and there's no better example of that than a slice of delicious cake. Since many of Tamriel's roots are best left to skilled alchemists, forgo the mandrake, corkbulb, and trama root in favor of the more familiar and safer carrots and parsnips.

LEVEL

Prep: 15 minutes **Baking:** 30 minutes **Makes:** 1 cake, about 8 large servings
Pairs well with: Hot Spiced Cider (page 169)

Cake:

½ cup (1 stick) unsalted butter, plus more for the pan

½ cup packed brown sugar

½ cup molasses

2 eggs

1 teaspoon vanilla extract

1 teaspoon Nord Spices (page 23)

1 teaspoon ground ginger

2 cups shredded carrot or parsnip

½ cup dried currants

1 teaspoon baking soda

½ teaspoon salt

2 cups all-purpose flour

Frosting:

1 cup cream cheese

¼ cup (½ stick) unsalted butter, softened

¾ cup powdered sugar

2 tablespoons honey

Dash of vanilla extract

Pinch of salt

Sliced almonds for garnishing (optional)

To make the cake:

1. Preheat the oven to 350°F and lightly butter the bottom and sides of an 8- or 9-inch round cake pan. Lightly dust with flour, then tap out any extra.

2. In a medium bowl, cream together the butter and brown sugar until light and fluffy. Mix in the molasses, eggs, vanilla, and Nord Spices. Stir in the grated carrot and dried currants, making sure everything is evenly distributed. Mix in the baking soda, salt, and flour until you have a nice thick batter. Pour this into the prepared pan and smooth out the top. Bake for about 30 minutes, until a toothpick inserted into the center of the cake comes out clean. Allow to cool in the pan for at least 15 minutes before flipping out of the pan onto a rack to finish cooling.

To make the frosting:

3. While the cake bakes, beat the cream cheese and butter together in a medium bowl until they are one smooth consistency. Gradually add in the powdered sugar, followed by the honey, vanilla, and salt. When the cake has cooled completely, spread the frosting over the top of the cake. Decorate with sliced almonds if you like, and a pinch of Nord Spices to finish.

SWEETROLLS

Don't let anyone steal your sweetroll ever again. Instead of
guarding your hard-won baked goods against bandits and that
pesky Thieves Guild, now you can bake them in the quiet safety of
your own home with no one the wiser.

LEVEL

Prep: 10 minutes **Rising:** 30 minutes **Baking:** 15 minutes
Makes: 4 good-sized rolls **Pairs with:** morning coffee or tea, breakfast sausage

Rolls:

3 tablespoons unsalted
   butter, melted

1 cup warm whole milk

2 tablespoons honey

Pinch of salt

1 egg

2 teaspoons active dry yeast

2 cups all-purpose flour

Frosting:

2 tablespoons cream cheese,
   softened

1 tablespoon unsalted butter,
   softened

½ cup powdered sugar

2 tablespoons heavy cream

To make the rolls:

1. Preheat the oven to 350°F. In a large bowl, combine the butter, warm milk, and honey, stirring until the honey has dissolved. Add the salt and yeast, followed by the egg and flour, and mix completely until you have a smooth batter. Spoon evenly into four 5-inch miniature Bundt pans. Allow to rise for just 30 minutes, then bake for 15 minutes, until a toothpick inserted in the rolls comes out clean.

To make the frosting:

2. While the rolls bake, cream together the cream cheese, butter, and powdered sugar in a small bowl. Gradually add just enough heavy cream to get a smooth, thick icing that barely runs off a spoon.

3. When the rolls are finished baking, allow to cool for 5 minutes in the pan, then tip out onto a cooling rack. When they are completely cooled, spoon the icing over the tops of the rolls, letting it run down the sides a little.

Firsthold

Cloudrest

Lillandril

Shimmerene

Alinor

Sunhhold

Dusk

Summerset Isle

DRINKS

QUICK MEADS

It's said that many a Nord's first nourishment is a nip of mead, even before tasting their mother's milk. Mead is in their blood as much as in their drinking horns, and everyone has his or her favorite variety. So grab your favorite drinking buddy; you'll be a lot happier and a lot warmer with some mead in your belly!

LEVEL

Prep: 10 minutes **Active time:** 15 minutes **Fermenting:** at least 3 months
Makes: ½ gallon **Pairs well with:** songs by the fire, a sense of adventure, a drinking horn

Basic Recipe:

2 cups honey

6 to 8 cups spring water

Additional ingredients, per recipe (see pages 162 to 165)

One packet ale yeast, about ¼ ounce

1. Pour the honey into a clean ½-gallon glass jug (a carboy). Bring 4 cups of the water to a boil, then pour the boiling water over the honey in the carboy and stir or swirl until the honey has dissolved. Add any additional ingredients, as listed for each recipe, then top off with the remaining 2 to 4 cups of cool water, leaving a few inches of space at the top. Let this mixture cool to room temperature, then add the yeast. Fix a brewing airlock to the top of the jug and set in a moderately warm place to begin fermenting.

2. After a day or so you should see tiny bubbles rising up to the surface. Let it ferment for a week, then taste. At the 2-week mark, the alcohol by volume (ABV) will be low, somewhat less than a light beer. This is a great time to strain out the extra ingredients and start enjoying the mead.

3. These meads are designed to be enjoyed while they are fairly young, while still cloudy with a bit of fizz to them. If you'd like to age them, you can leave them in the carboys to continue fermenting for several months until the sediment drops and the mead becomes clear. The final ABV at that point should be around 10 percent.

| TIP |

The Honningbrew Mead adapts especially well to longer aging, while the Black-Briar Mead is better early while still fruity, and it's no wonder—the Honningbrew has set out to make an excellent mead, while the Black-Briars are out for profit alone. In the end, just remember that meads are a lot like fishwives: The older they are, the less sweetness is left.

Local honey is always the best choice for making mead, and it's hard to go wrong with a wildflower variety. However, if you would like to play some with the ingredients, try different varietals of honey and see what goes well with each mead. For instance, orange blossom honey will impart a delicate citrus flavor.

HONNINGBREW MEAD

Known throughout Skyrim as the finest mead outside of Sovngarde, Honningbrew's reputation is well deserved. Pulling ingredients from their own hives and the surrounding meadows, Sabjorn has crafted a perfectly balanced brew that pleases revelers far and wide. Except near Riften, of course . . .

Additional Ingredients:

1 tablespoon culinary
  lavender

½ red apple

1 inch fresh ginger, peeled
  and sliced thin

BLACK-BRIAR MEAD

Although the recipe has been closely guarded, everything has a price. The honey comes from the Goldenglow Estate, and when combined with the other ingredients makes a fruity mead that's a little dark and moody, just like the entire Black-Briar family.

Additional Ingredients:

6 ounces crushed blackberries

1 to 2 tablespoons dried rosehips

½ teaspoon ground cloves

1 cinnamon stick

Dash of salt

JUNIPER BERRY MEAD

Though Vilod has joined his ancestors, his mead lives
on in Helgen and beyond. Using the native juniper berry
and red mountain flowers, he created a mead that truly
embodies the spirit of Skyrim.

TIP

Dried yarrow and hibiscus flowers can often be found in health food stores or at
co-ops in the bulk food section.

Additional Ingredients:

2 tablespoons crushed juniper
berries

2 teaspoons dried yarrow

1 tablespoon dried hibiscus
flowers

NORD MEAD

Like all meads made at home rather than at the commercial meaderies, this recipe varies from clan to clan, village to town. But all Nords agree that it has to have certain characteristics: warming, heavy on the spices, and refreshing.

Additional Ingredients:

½ teaspoon ground cardamom

1 inch fresh ginger, peeled and sliced thin

Zest of 1 orange, avoiding the rind

1 teaspoon whole cloves

1 cinnamon stick

IMPERIAL MULLED WINE

Many Imperials have found Skyrim's climate difficult to bear, so when one enterprising garrison cook whipped up this hot drink to help ward off the northern chill, it quickly gained popularity across the region and beyond. It makes use of a few Imperial ingredients that must be imported, but its warming qualities are well worth the extra expense.

LEVEL

Prep: 10 minutes **Makes:** 2 servings
Pairs well with: Stewed Apples and Eidar Cheese (page 63), sharp cheese and dried meats

2½ cups white wine

1 teaspoon Imperial
    Seasoning (page 27)

1 cinnamon stick

1 bay leaf

1 tablespoon sugar or more
    to taste

1. Combine all ingredients in a small pot over medium heat. Bring the wine up to just under a simmer, so it is steaming but not bubbling. Keep it there for around 10 minutes to allow the flavors to combine, then strain into clean heat-proof glasses.

 TIP

This recipe can be scaled up easily depending on how many soldiers you need to keep warm. Securing the spices in a tea strainer can also help keep the drink clear.

HOT SPICED CIDER

Both the red and green apples of Skyrim are used widely in cooking, both for their juice and for the fruit itself. This drink is popular among children and those who had just a little too much of the strong stuff the night before.

LEVEL

Prep: 15 minutes **Makes:** 2 servings
Pairs well with: Spiced Root Cake (page 155)

3 cups apple cider

1 tablespoon coriander seed, crushed and measured

2 tablespoons juniper berries, crushed and measured

2 or 3 cinnamon sticks

Brown sugar, honey, or maple syrup for serving

1. Combine the cider, coriander, juniper berries, and cinnamon sticks in a small saucepan and place over-medium low heat. Allow the cider to blend with the flavors for 10 to 15 minutes, never letting it boil. Strain into clean mugs and sweeten with brown sugar, honey, or maple syrup to taste.

 TIP

For a stronger flavor, cover the pot off the heat and let sit overnight to infuse, then strain and reheat to serve.

SAN'S SPICED WINE

Although the exact recipe for San's Spiced Wine remains a closely guarded secret, a more unscrupulous adventurer can find the list of spices in the logs of the East Empire Trading Company. And if you happen to be out on a chilly evening to see the burning of King Olaf in Solitude, it'll put a little fire in your veins.

LEVEL

Prep: 15 minutes   **Steeping:** 12 hours
Makes: about 6 servings   **Pairs well with:** Festival Hand Pies (page 119)

One 750-ml bottle red wine, such as Cabernet

2 cinnamon sticks

¼ teaspoon ground cardamom

1 teaspoon crushed juniper berries

1 inch fresh ginger, peeled and sliced thin

Pinch of ground pepper

2 tablespoons brown sugar

2 shots brandy

1 shot port

1. Combine all ingredients except the brandy and port in a large saucepan over medium-low heat, and bring up to just under a simmer. Keep at this heat for about 15 minutes, until the sugar has dissolved and the mixture smells fragrant. Remove from heat and let sit overnight at room temperature, covered, or for at least 12 hours.

2. Add the brandy and port, then strain into clean bottles. Enjoy warm or at room temperature.

SKOOMA

Because skooma is so highly sought-after, yet so illegal, some enterprising innkeepers across Tamriel have cooked up their own version of a cordial that mimics that addictively sweet drink so loved by the Khajiit.

LEVEL

Prep: 10 minutes **Infusing:** at least 2 to 3 weeks **Makes:** 1 small bottle
Pairs well with: Spiced Root Cake (page 155), fresh yogurt, ice cream

1 cup sugar

¾ cup boiling water

2 cups vodka

10 pitted dried apricots, diced

Pinch of ground cardamom

Dash of vanilla extract

1. Combine the sugar and boiling water in a small heat-proof container, and stir until the sugar has dissolved. Pour into a clean bottle, then add the remaining ingredients. Cap the bottle and sit somewhere dim to infuse, shaking occasionally.

2. Allow to steep for 2 to 3 weeks, or up to 1 month for maximum flavor. Strain out the apricots and store the skooma in a glass bottle. serve in small cordial glasses.

SNOWBERRY CORDIAL

This easy-to-make cordial has become a staple of hospitality among Nords, as it is commonly offered to guests and family in small glasses as a welcome warming nip and in bottles as a gift.

LEVEL

Prep: 15 minutes   **Steeping:** 24 hours
Makes: 7 servings   **Pairs well with:** rich fruitcake, evenings by the fire

One 750-ml bottle inexpensive red wine, like a Cabernet

1 cup water

2 cups sugar

12 ounces whole fresh cranberries

¼ cup dried rosehips

1 cinnamon stick

1½ cups brandy

1. In a large pot, combine the wine, water, sugar, cranberries, rosehips, and cinnamon stick. Increase the heat to medium-high, and cook until the cranberries start popping. Remove the from heat and roughly mash the berries with a potato masher. Cover the pot and allow to sit at room temperature for about 24 hours.

2. Strain out the berries and cinnamon stick, then add the brandy. Store in airtight bottles for up to several months. Serve in small glasses.

> **TIP**
>
> Try a splash of this cordial in lemonade during warmer seasons.

SPICED WARM MILK WITH HONEY

Most Khajiit have taken to making this recipe with moonsugar in place of the honey, and some even add a splash of skooma; while it's not recommended for non-Khajiit races, it certainly works wonders as a nightcap for them. For everyone else, it's still a warming drink first thing in the morning or right before bed.
Go on, nobody needs to know you're a milk drinker.

LEVEL

Prep: 5 minutes **Makes:** 1 large serving **Pairs well with:** Braided Bread (page 71)

2 cups whole milk

Dash of vanilla extract

½ teaspoon Nord Spices (page 23), plus more for garnish

1 to 2 tablespoons honey

Whipped cream for topping (optional)

1. Combine the milk, vanilla, and Nord Spices in a small pot over medium heat. Heat the milk until it's steaming but just shy of bubbling, then stir in honey to taste. Pour into a heat-proof mug and top with whipped cream and a pinch of Nord Spices to garnish.

SWEET NOG

This thick, boozy, protein-filled beverage is just the thing to welcome you in from the cold after a day of hard labor. It's a popular warming drink, especially at homesteads where flocks of chickens provide a constant source of eggs. A more enterprising adventurer might use pine thrush eggs, but they're harder to find.

LEVEL

Prep: 15 minutes **Makes:** 6 to 8 servings
Pairs well with: Birch Cookies (page 137)

6 egg yolks

1 teaspoon vanilla extract

¼ cup packed brown sugar

½ teaspoon Nord Spices (page 23)

One 14-ounce can sweetened condensed milk

½ cup brandy

1 cup whole milk

1. Combine all ingredients in a medium bowl set over a pot of simmering water. Whisk gently for 5 to 10 minutes to cook the yolks and while the mixture thickens noticeably. The nog will thicken more as it chills, so if the mixture is too thick, add a little extra milk until you have the consistency you prefer.

2. Pour into a glass bottle and let the nog cool before refrigerating. Chilled, it should keep for up to a week. Can be served room temperature or warm in small glasses.

CANIS ROOT TEA

A favorite drink of eccentric mages across Tamriel, this tea turns the gnarled canis root into a richly flavored beverage that wakes up both body and mind. If you can't find a good steward, this recipe will help you make a perfect cup of tea yourself, assuming you aren't above such menial tasks.

LEVEL

Prep: 5 minutes   **Cooking:** 15 minutes   **Makes:** 1 serving
Pairs well with: gingerbread cookies, Spiced Root Cake (page 155)

1 tablespoon dried
   dandelion root

1 tablespoon dried burdock
   root

2½ cups water

1 cinnamon stick

Cream and brown sugar for
   serving

1. Toast the dried dandelion and burdock root in a small saucepan over medium heat for about 5 minutes, or until darkening in color and fragrant. Add the water to the pan along with the cinnamon stick. Simmer for about 15 minutes, then strain into a heat-proof mug. Add cream and brown sugar to taste.

RED MOUNTAIN FLOWER TEA

Gathered along roadsides throughout Skyrim, these flowers are valued by alchemists for their magicka properties. But the common folk also frequently collect some for a refreshing tea while on their way to and from town. True Nords drink it unsweetened, enjoying the tartness the flowers lend the tea.

LEVEL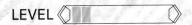

Prep: 5 minutes **Steeping:** at least 4 hours **Makes:** 1 serving
Pairs well with: Long Taffy Treat (page 141), Apple Cobbler (page 149)

¼ cup dried hibiscus flowers

Pinch of Nord Spices
   (page 23)

A few slices of peeled fresh
   ginger

2 cups boiling water

Sugar or honey for serving

1. Combine the hibiscus, Nord Spices, ginger, and boiling water in a heat-proof container and let steep for at least 4 hours. Strain into a clean mug and sweeten with sugar or honey to taste.

WATER OF LIFE

Considered something of a cure-all by many Nords, this potent beverage is reputed to bring the ill back up to full health. Everyone seems to have their own family recipe, but I managed to wheedle this one out of a farmer in Falkreath.

LEVEL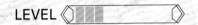

Prep: 5 minutes **Steeping:** 3 days
Makes: 1 batch, about 4 cups **Pairs well with:** best on its own, after a full meal

2 teaspoons fennel seeds

2 teaspoons caraway seeds

1 tablespoon juniper berries

1 sprig fresh dill

4 cups vodka

1. In a small sauté pan or skillet over medium heat, toast the fennel and caraway seeds for several minutes until they are lightly browned and smell fragrant. Add the seeds and the remaining ingredients to a large jug and seal the top.

2. Let steep for 2 to 3 days, until it turns a light golden color and has as strong a flavor as you like. Serve in small glasses. It can be sipped as a digestive or knocked back for a more medicinal approach.

DIETARY CONSIDERATIONS

v = Vegetarian v+ = Vegan GF = Gluten-free
v*, v+*, & GF* = Easily made vegetarian, vegan, or gluten-free with simple alterations

BASICS

Custard Sauce	V		GF
Imperial Mushroom Sauce	V*		GF*
Rustic Mustard	V	V+*	GF
Rye Pie Dough	V		GF*
Snowberry Sauce	V	V+	GF
Spiced Butter	V		GF
Spices, Seasonings, & Condiments	V	V+	GF
Sweet Crostata Dough	V		GF*

SIDES, STARTERS, & SNACKS

Argonian Swamp Shrimp Boil			GF
Baby Carrots in Moonsugar Glaze	V	V+*	GF
Baked Ash Yams	V		GF
Bosmer Bites			GF
Double-Baked Potatoes	V		GF
Grilled Leeks	V	V+*	GF
Hot Mudcrab Dip			GF
Leek and Cheese Crostata	V		GF*
Mushroom and Vegetable Risotto	V	V+*	GF
Redguard Rice			
Saltrice Porridge	V	V+*	GF
Stewed Apples and Eidar Cheese	V		GF
Sunlight Soufflé	V		GF*

BAKED GOODS

Braided Bread	V		
Cabbage Biscuits	V	V+*	GF*
Cheese Scones	V		
Garlic Bread	V		
Lavender and Honey Bread	V		
Meadow Rye Bread	V		
Nut and Seed Loaf	V		GF
Rye Crisps	V	V+	
S'jirra's Famous Potato Bread	V		

SOUPS & STEWS

Apple Cabbage Stew			GF
Braised Rib Stew with Farro			GF*
Coastal Clam Chowder			GF*
Pea Soup	V*	V+*	GF
Potage le Magnifique	V*	V+*	GF*
Potato Cheddar Soup	V*		GF*
Vegetable Soup	V	V+*	GF*

MAIN COURSES

Baked White River Salmon			
Chicken Dumplings			
Companions Meatball Bake			GF
Elsweyr Fondue	V		GF
Festival Hand Pies			
Goatherd's Pie			GF*
Horker Loaf			GF*
Juniper Lamb Chops			GF
Kwama Egg Quiche	V		GF*
Orsimer Venison			GF
Seared Nordic Barnacles	V		GF

DESSERTS

Apple Cobbler	V		GF*
Birch Cookies	V		
Boiled Creme Treat	V		
Honey Nut Treat	V	V+	GF
Honey Pudding	V		GF
Honeycomb Brittle	V		GF
Long Taffy Treat	V		GF
Oatmeal Raisin Shortbread	V		
Sheogorath's Strawberry Tarts	V		GF*
Snowberry Crostata	V		GF*
Spiced Root Cake	V		GF*
Sweetrolls	V		

DRINKS

Canis Root Tea	V	V+	GF
Hot Spiced Cider	V	V+	GF
Imperial Mulled Wine	V	V+	GF
Quick Meads	V		GF
Red Mountain Flower Tea	V	V+	GF
San's Spiced Wine	V	V+	GF
Skooma	V	V+	GF
Snowberry Cordial	V	V+	GF
Spiced Warm Milk with Honey	V	V+*	GF
Sweet Nog	V		GF
Water of Life	V	V+	GF

MEASUREMENT CONVERSION CHARTS

VOLUME

US	METRIC
⅕ teaspoon (tsp)	1 ml
1 teaspoon (tsp)	5 ml
1 tablespoon (tbsp)	15 ml
1 fluid ounce (fl. oz.)	30 ml
⅕ cup	50 ml
¼ cup	60 ml
⅓ cup	80 ml
3.4 fluid ounces (fl. oz.)	100 ml
½ cup	120 ml
⅔ cup	160 ml
¾ cup	180 ml
1 cup	240 ml
1 pint (2 cups)	480 ml
1 quart (4 cups)	.95 liter

WEIGHT

US	METRIC
0.5 ounces (oz.)	14 grams (g)
1 ounce (oz.)	28 grams (g)
¼ pound (lb)	113 grams (g)
⅓ pound (lb)	151 grams (g)
½ pound (lb)	227 grams (g)
1 pound (lb)	454 grams (g)

TEMPERATURES

FAHRENHEIT	CELSIUS
200°	93.3°
212°	100°
250°	120°
275°	135°
300°	150°
325°	165°
350°	177°
400°	205°
425°	220°
450°	233°
475°	245°
500°	260°

TITAN
BOOKS

144 Southwark Street
London SE1 0UP
www.titanbooks.com

Find us on Facebook: www.facebook.com/TitanBooks
Follow us on Twitter: @TitanBooks

Published by arrangement with Insight Editions, San Rafael, California, in 2019.
www.insighteditions.com

A CIP catalogue record for this title is available from the British Library.

ISBN: 978-1-78909-067-3

Publisher: Raoul Goff
Associate Publisher: Vanessa Lopez
Creative Director: Chrissy Kwasnik
Designers: Yousef Ghorbani and Evelyn Furuta
Senior Editor: Amanda Ng
Editorial Assistant: Maya Alpert
Production Editors: Rachel Anderson and Jennifer Bentham
Production Manager: Sadie Crofts

ROOTS of PEACE   REPLANTED PAPER

Insight Editions, in association with Roots of Peace, will plant two trees for each tree
used in the manufacturing of this book. Roots of Peace is an internationally renowned
humanitarian organization dedicated to eradicating land mines worldwide and
converting war-torn lands into productive farms and wildlife habitats. Roots of Peace
will plant two million fruit and nut trees in Afghanistan and provide farmers there with
the skills and support necessary for sustainable land use.

Manufactured in China by Insight Editions

10 9 8 7 6 5

Northpoint Farrun Solitude

Jelhana Morthal

Sharnhelm Markarth

High Rock Evermor Dragonstar

Wayrest Skaven Bluhir

Hammerfell Falk

Daggerfall

Sentinel Chor

The Alik'r Desert

Gilane Janeth Cyro

Hegathe

Rihad

Stros M'Kai Anvil Kvatch

The Abecean Sea Arenth

Firsthold

Falinesti

Zillandril Cloudrest Silvenar

Skywatch Valenwood

Shimmerene Woodhearth Elden Root

Alinor Greenheart

Sunhold Dusk Southpoint

N

Summerset Isle

The Etheric Ocean

The Empire of Tamriel